This book is dedicated to all those who suffer because the world has told them that they must have that which is of no worth and which will keep them from peace. May you find comfort here.

Wherefore, do not spend money for that which is of no worth, nor your labor for that which cannot satisfy. Hearken diligently unto me, and remember the words which I have spoken; and come unto the Holy One of Israel, and feast upon that which perisheth not, neither can be corrupted, and let your soul delight in fatness. —2 NEPHI 9:51

CONFRONTING THE MYTH OF SELF-ESTEEM

CONFRONTING THE MYTH OF SELF-ESTEEM

TWELVE KEYS TO FINDING PEACE

ESTER RASBAND

Deseret Book Company
Salt Lake City, Utah

Library of Congress Cataloging-in-Publication Data

Rasband, Ester.
Confronting the myth of self-esteem : twelve keys to finding peace / Ester Rasband.
p. cm.
Includes bibliographical references and index.
ISBN 1-57345-381-1 (pbk.)
1. Spiritual life—Church of Jesus Christ of Latter-day Saints. 2. Self-esteem—Religious aspects—Church of Jesus Christ of Latter-day Saints. 3. Church of Jesus Christ of Latter-day Saints—Doctrines. I. Title.
BX8656.R366 1998
248.4'89332—dc21

98-25905
CIP

Printed in the United States of America

21239-6368

10 9 8 7 6 5 4 3 2

Contents

PART 4

THE KEYS OF CHOICE

PART 5

ADDITIONAL THOUGHTS

Acknowledgments

To those whose stories I tell here, I thank you for what you taught me. If my lessons were learned at your expense, I beg your forgiveness. May you all take satisfaction in recognizing that you have moved me forward toward peace.

This book has been a product of my deep conviction and a labor of passion that often required the objectivity of others. I want to thank Linda Gundry of Deseret Book as well as Leslie Stitt, my brother Clyde Johnson, and my son, Jim Rasband, for significant editing helps. I'm also grateful to those who struggled through and identified weaknesses in early drafts of the manuscript, including our missionaries Bryce Tingle, Craig Teuscher, and Jennifer Nelson Lloyd; my former colleague, Larry Beall; my friends LaVonne VanOrden and Darlene Burns; and my sons and their wives: Jim and Mary and Win and Kelley Rasband. To my friend Nancy Richardson I owe a debt for the gift of her precious time. I thank Dave Trebas for his creative input.

Most of all, I thank my husband, Jim, who challenged every word as it went to paper at the same time that he provided a climate of love that made it possible for me to proceed.

Introduction

Friends often ask me, "What project are you working on these days?" Lately my answer has been, "An anti–self-esteem book." Friends laugh, then offer their own unique responses. I get everything from "Good!" or "Wonderful!" to "How can anybody be *anti*–self-esteem?"

I generally add a sort of disclaimer: "It's not confidence that I'm against. It's self-esteem, or at least, the *search* for self-esteem."

Now, before you close this book in exasperation, let me explain. I really believe that the two concepts, confidence and self-esteem, have come to have quite different meanings. Genuine feelings of confidence and worth are important to our feeling peace and joy, but these feelings can't be found by desperately seeking something we call self-esteem. And self-esteem, with its focus on *self,* is a different story from genuine confidence. That difference is what this book is about.

Deep down all of us know our mortal limitations. We know we aren't wonderful—our enormous, eternal potential notwithstanding. Inadequacy is the human condition, and unless we tap into the adequacy of our Father in Heaven, we live in a somewhat fearful state: fearful that our inadequacy will cause us to fail and will stand in the way of our being loved and valued. Society, trying to rid us of that fear, tells us that we must feel adequate in *ourselves*. This emphasis on self-esteem, however, only masks our fears, and unfortunately it concentrates these fears instead of casting them out.

I think the belief that we must have self-esteem exacerbates the very problem it's supposed to combat: our search for self-esteem is a depressant, an anxiety producer, and a dreadful pressure. Genuine confidence, on the other hand, is a byproduct of our accomplishment and the Savior's atonement—a combination of what we do with God's help, and what God has done for us.

You might ask, as some of my friends have, "But isn't some self-esteem necessary to achieve, to accomplish things? Isn't self-esteem the means?"

"Not self-esteem," I answer. "Just love. Love brings peace, and peace leads to confidence."

"Well, isn't loving yourself the same as having self-esteem?"

"Yes. But I'm not talking about self-love. I'm talking about something else entirely."

These philosophical conversations engross me, and others' insights always provide enlightenment. Someone is sure to mention what a relief from loneliness it must be when one's faith is in God instead of in oneself. The responsibility to be confident all on our own, we admit, is too heavy to bear.

Our conclusion is always that there is no anxiety in seeking first the kingdom of God and his righteousness. There is no distress in loving God with all our heart, might, mind, and strength and in serving his other children because we love *him* (and them.).[1] Confidence, we conclude, is the natural result of that kind of loving quest. The torment comes about when we

1. See Matt. 6:33, "But seek ye first the kingdom of God, and his righteousness; and all these things shall be added unto you." See also Amos 5:4; Ezra 8:22; 1 Chron. 16:10–11; and Jer. 45:5, which reads, "Seekest thou great things for thyself? seek them not."

buy into the belief of society that we must first seek our own *self* and serve *it.* The worldly theory is that when we find *ourselves* all else will be added unto us.

But it seems to me that the gospel teaches us that when we *stop looking* for ourselves, God can add all else unto us. It is the *search* for self-esteem that tortures us, not our lack of it. If we could stop "seeking our own," as Paul identified it in 1 Corinthians 13:5, we could get rid of the feeling that we live in a vice.

The search for self-esteem will always frustrate us. In fact, only the most complete humility will ultimately bring confidence.[2] It is perfect irony that that which our worldly self would prize most highly—feeling good about ourselves—can only be achieved by facing that which our worldly self would tell us we must never face: our nothingness. It has been called the Christian paradox: We must forget ourselves and concentrate on the greatness of God.[3] Then, and only then, will we find ourselves.[4]

Reassuringly, my conversations with my friends usually end with the understanding that genuine confidence doesn't come to us overnight and that no one achieves it perfectly in this life. Nevertheless, the forerunner to confidence is *peace,* and peace *is* available in this life.[5]

---

2. "And whosoever shall exalt himself shall be abased; and he that shall humble himself shall be exalted" (Matt. 23:12). See also Ezek. 21:26; Matt. 5:5; D&C 124:114.

3. "Even so I would that ye should remember, and always retain in remembrance, the greatness of God, and your own nothingness, and his goodness and long-suffering towards you, unworthy creatures, and humble yourselves even in the depths of humility, calling on the name of the Lord daily, and standing steadfastly in the faith of that which is to come, which was spoken by the mouth of the angel" (Mosiah 4:11). See also Hel. 12: 7–26; Mosiah 4:5, 9.

4. JST, Matt. 10:34.

5. "But learn that he who doeth the works of righteousness shall receive his reward, even peace in this world, and eternal life in the world to come" (D&C 59:23).

The world today, seeing that we are fearful, teaches that what we need is self-esteem. I think, however, that the world has made an error in identification. *Peace* is what the heart of man genuinely craves—peace born of love. That peaceful feeling of acknowledging that we are loved is what makes it possible to grow and contribute. Peace born of love is what gives mankind the strength to make effort and the reassurance to have patience.

The scriptures teach that peace comes only from the Prince of Peace. The search for self-esteem becomes an obstacle to our finding the comfort of the Lord's love and grace. Peace is what I pray that together we can find.

PART 1

The Keys to Understanding

"And seekest thou great things for thyself? seek them not."

—Jeremiah 45:5

"And the Lord gave them rest round about."

—2 Chronicles 15:15

THE FIRST KEY

Accept God's Word as the Ultimate Instruction Manual

"He that exalteth himself shall be abased, and he that abaseth himself shall be exalted" (D&C 101:42). I read aloud the scripture from the Doctrine and Covenants and set the volume down on the table. I was preparing to give a Relief Society lesson, and I wanted to make certain I taught this principle correctly. For a few minutes I explored the meaning of the word *abase* as defined in *Webster's Ninth Collegiate Dictionary:* "To lower physically. To lower in rank, office, prestige, or esteem. . . . To lower in one's own estimation or in that of others. *Abase* suggests losing or voluntarily yielding up dignity or prestige."[1]

As I studied the lesson, I recalled many verses that underline this basic truth. This is what the Sermon on the Mount was all about—meekness, abasing oneself before the Lord (see Matt. 5:1–12).

Later, as I presented the lesson in Relief Society, I stopped

1. *Webster's Ninth New Collegiate Dictionary* (Springfield, Mass.: Merriam Webster, Inc., 1983), 43.

for a moment and looked at the sisters. I could see that there were some anxious feelings. Abasement—profound humility—is an uncomfortable, confusing topic in today's world.

"That's all well and good scripturally," one sister said, "but in terms of human development, it's another matter."

Comments came from all over the room. No hands were raised, just voices.

"Self-esteem is so important!"

"I think humility just means being willing to keep the commandments."

"*Abasement* is such a strong word!"

"We have a whole body of research that we need to add to our scriptural knowledge," said the sister who had begun the discussion. "We have learned a great deal about human development."

I was quiet for a moment. I didn't fully understand all the significance and ramifications of abasing ourselves. But I knew that the scriptures are, so to speak, the Lord's instruction manual for us. Finally I said, "I can't resolve for you all the contradictions you see in the search for self-esteem. I only know that the Lord's instructions are to abase ourselves. This much more I know: the goal of human development is eternal life, and peace comes through seeking this goal.

"God will help us understand these things, but our secular knowledge must conform to what we learn in his precious gift of the scriptures. Not vice versa."

There are many instruction manuals in competition with God's own—almost limitless numbers of man-made volumes on various aspects of "human development." More self-help books are published than any other kind. How dearly we want peace for ourselves and for each other. How quick we are to try to give one another "peace made simple" and "peace without pain." It is our nature to provide bookstores full of new and fashionable "bodies of research," and it is our nature to be an eager market for them as well. Abasement is too . . . well, too humiliating. Self-esteem seems, at first glance, to be the more agreeable way. Oh, how important it is to look beyond the first glance—to look to the scriptures, which are the Lord's instruction manual, and find not peace made simple, but peace made possible—not peace without pain but peace that overcomes pain.

That night I found a scripture I hadn't really read in the same way before. I knew it was given me as a reassurance that God has all wisdom and that our "bodies of research" must meet the test of agreement with his word—not just excerpts of his word, either, but all of it. The verse was Job 21:22, which reads, "Shall any teach God knowledge? seeing he judgeth those that are high."

THE SECOND KEY

Stand Ready to Sacrifice Your Self-Esteem

For weeks after that Relief Society lesson I thought of little else. I suppose I would have to say that this book was born that Sunday morning. The birth, however, followed a long gestation period, which was in turn preceded by a significant period of infertility.

Twenty-some-odd years ago, for a youth conference, I remember making badges for every attendee. The bright and shiny stickers were decorated with ribbons and declared, "I Am Lovable and Capable!"

Although I am sure our love for those young people carried the day, I am now equally sure that the power of suggestion did not change their self-image but instead caused some stress. Nevertheless, I was more into self-help than divine help in those days, and I did indeed believe that what they thought about themselves was the most important and most fundamental facet of their development. Moreover, I believed that *I* could give them confidence. The years passed without much change in my understanding.

Although small and fleeting experiences were preparing

the lining of my heart to receive the doctrine of grace and humility, I remember one important episode that could be identified as the seed. My husband was presiding in the Canada Montreal Mission and I had planned a sisters' conference. I was aware of what could only be called ill feelings between the sisters and the elders, and my husband and I decided to talk with the missionaries about the differences between men and women in the hopes that their understanding one another would ease the tension. He spoke with the elders and I spoke with the sisters.

"Men," I began, "get their self-esteem from their workplace. Though there are exceptions, they are often more task-oriented than women are, because their accomplishments in the workplace determine their good feelings. Women, on the other hand, generally (again, with exceptions) get their self-esteem from relationships—from nurturing others, from making others happy."

We talked then about how those differences created variations in the proselyting styles of sisters and elders and why we couldn't judge the men's priesthood leadership by our framework. We talked of the collisions that often come from the innate differences between men and women.

But the sisters weren't buying it.

"It's more righteous to nurture others!" They were adamant. "To treat investigators as a 'task' is in violation of the second great commandment!" "It's sinful to get your self-esteem that way!"

I told them that our discussion was for the purpose of understanding, not changing, one another. We left the topic, but it was obviously not resolved, and I suffered much discontent over the entire issue. There followed a night of prayer and sleeplessness.

The next morning, as I lay in bed, I had a burst of clear

understanding that I felt had been given me by the Spirit. It was the first crack in the shell of my faith in self-esteem. I was excited with all the possible implications. I sat right down at the computer and wrote a letter to all the sisters. Here is the gist of that letter:

> Dear Sisters:
>
> I figured out what was wrong with our discussion about the differences between men and women: it was based on observations of the differences between the way that men and women get their self-esteem.
>
> Although my explanation was meant to explain and not excuse behaviors, I was assuming that getting self-esteem was paramount and therefore necessarily good. You were right, of course, that such logic can lead to sin. This life is not about getting self-esteem. It is about learning to love and to obey.
>
> While men, in fueling their self-esteem, might choose to give up loving to get the job done, they must fight that tendency if they would prepare themselves for eternal life—even if it means giving up a little self-esteem.
>
> Women on the other hand, who might prefer to de-emphasize the task in favor of the loving, must learn to get the job done even if it means not being able to have everyone happy all the time. Love must come out of obedience, and obedience must come out of love if we are to prepare ourselves to live with our Father in Heaven someday. All of us must be prepared to give up a little self-esteem to do what is right.
>
> The Lord has promised us that if we are willing to make that sacrifice, we will end up with more good feelings about ourselves than we could ever have had by trying to create that confidence within ourselves. That is the meaning of the Christian paradox, that we must lose ourselves to find ourselves.

"Let thy bowels also be full of charity towards all men, and to the household of faith, and let virtue garnish thy thoughts unceasingly; then shall thy confidence wax strong in the presence of God; and the doctrine of the priesthood shall distil upon thy soul as the dews from heaven" (D&C 121:45).

Still, it is valuable—in the interest of love itself—to learn to understand one another's "natural man." That is what empathy is all about. Empathy may be helpful in leadership, and empathetic leadership may cause another of God's children to want to overcome his own natural man.

The important thing is to learn to sacrifice those sources of worldly self-esteem for the benefit of others. That sacrifice is a great key to eternal life. Paul was trying to help us understand that key when he so often emphasized that it is unacceptable to "seek one's own" (see 1 Cor. 13:5; Philip. 2:3). Self-esteem must be the sacrifice that we lay on the altar.

Ultimately, a great and marvelous self-esteem will be a gift from God to those who do not seek it—who diligently lose themselves in his service. Diligence is, after all, a matter of honesty. We know if we are being all we can be. It is, as one sister said, a matter between you and the Lord. No excuses. No judgments of others. Just honesty and two-way love. We must be willing to lay our self-esteem at the feet of the Lord and seek instead to love him and obey him.

Thank you for this wonderful experience with the gospel that we are having together. You continue to teach me much.

Love, Sister Rasband

That was the beginning of my understanding.

After that I was drawn to more reading on the subject than I had ever done. It's hard to guess when and by whom the term *self-esteem* was coined. I learned it had been used as far back as the seventeenth century. Milton, through the mouth of an angel in *Paradise Lost,* said:

> Ofttimes nothing profits more
> Than self-esteem, grounded on just and right
> Well managed.

I see Milton's lines as implying that even three hundred years ago, there was need for caution in the search for self-esteem. Milton was flashing a yellow light: self-esteem must be grounded on integrity and carefully managed. He was evidently struggling with the concept and its application.

We hear the "self-esteem problem" labeled as a twentieth-century phenomenon, and many think of it as peculiarly American. Obviously that is not true. I believe that, no matter when the current naming was first used, the problem of searching for self-esteem is older than man himself; it started with Satan and caused a war in heaven. It is a universal facet of the natural man.

Perhaps the twentieth-century American contribution to the search has been that self-esteem is now seen as a right, and caution regarding its grounding and its management has been thrown to the winds. David G. Myers reports that in the self-ranking invited by the College Board, high school seniors taking their aptitude tests evaluate themselves quite surprisingly. In one year, out of 829,000 respondents, 70 percent rated themselves above average in terms of leadership ability and only 2 percent rated themselves below average. In the ability to get along with others 0 percent rated themselves below average, 60 percent rated themselves in the top 10 percent, and 25 percent saw themselves among the top 1 percent![1] Doubt-

---

1. David G. Myers, *The Inflated Self* (New York: The Seabury Press, 1980), 23–24.

less these statistics represent a considerable amount of resumé padding, since the respondents are intending to influence college admissions committees. Nevertheless, the numbers are staggering, and I mention them not to show that I believe these to be the true self-images of these young people but because they demonstrate a lack of inhibition in self-evaluation that is not only acceptable in our society but encouraged.

While the feeling of self-esteem was once considered something that must be restrained, the search for self-esteem is now given preeminence. We live in an age when we are told, in essence, that our problem is not in whether or not we are valuable, but whether or not we *believe* we are valuable. Focusing therefore on ourselves, we see little else. As the College Board respondents show, it becomes a distorted (and often counterfeit) view—one, I'm sure, that is not accompanied by peace and security. Deep inside we all feel our inadequacies—it's just that, in today's world, it is not okay to acknowledge them.

While Milton acknowledged the value of self-esteem founded in "just and right," I would suggest that when it is founded in just and right it is not self-esteem at all. It is the *confidence* the Lord refers to in the Doctrine and Covenants, wherein we are counseled to "let virtue garnish thy thoughts unceasingly; then shall thy confidence wax strong" (D&C 121:45). It's interesting that the words following this promise of confidence dwell on the priesthood: "And the doctrine of the priesthood shall distil upon thy soul as the dews from heaven." Could that be analogous to what Milton meant by self-esteem "well managed"?

As I studied the baffling and plentiful writings on self-esteem, the more I read of secular things, the more I found myself concentrating on the scriptures. I began to see how placing importance on self-esteem itself instead of on the "just and right" and its "management" has evolved into mass selfishness in every age. When we believe we must feel worthy in and of ourselves to think well of ourselves, we look skeptically at the need for growth: it threatens our self-satisfaction. We must not look up to others, because we can't consider ourselves any less. We must not give ourselves constructively critical evaluation, because we must believe we deserve life's rewards just as we are. Preoccupied with the self's status quo, we eschew growth and therefore forfeit progress toward eternal life. Peace doesn't come. Insecurity remains.

No, preoccupation with self is not a new phenomenon—else why would the scriptures deal with it so extensively? It is only that now, with the self-esteem ethic so widely accepted, the natural next step, that of self-absorption, has been legitimized. Legitimate or not, it is destructive. What the scriptures teach repeatedly and strongly is that while we search for self-esteem, peace and confidence will elude us. "Just and right" grounding comes only when we obediently rely on the Lord for strength and take our security from the Atonement. It is a byproduct of following him. Whether we believe we can earn our well-being, or simply lay claim to it, we are wrong. The scriptures teach that "without me ye can do nothing" (John 15:5). Peace and confidence are gifts from God, and they are gifts given only when we are willing to give up our self-esteem and approach him in total humility: "He that exalteth himself shall be abased, and he that abaseth himself shall be exalted" (D&C 101:42).

THE THIRD KEY

Identify the Needs of Your Heart

The power of suggestion is great, but in the end, not great enough. We believe we must have self-esteem, so we tell ourselves that we are splendid just the way we are. Deep down inside each of us, however, is the gnawing knowledge that belies what we're trying to tell ourselves. Our imperfection is all too real, and trying to maintain an image that is not based on that reality is intensely stressful. There comes a still, small voice telling us that there is something we must do to relieve that anxiety. Because we do not have a clear identification of our need, we think that we must do something to shore up our image of ourselves. The imperfection remains. The stress spirals upward.

That golden grain of divine discontent is not telling us that we must do something so that we can feel great about *ourselves.* I believe it is there to remind us that we must do something to show our humility to our Father in Heaven, so that we can feel great about *him.*

C. S. Lewis expresses the feeling especially well in his book *Mere Christianity:*

> If you really get into any kind of touch with Him you will, in fact, be humble—delightedly humble, feeling the infinite relief of having for once got rid of all the silly nonsense about your own dignity which has made you restless and unhappy all your life. He is trying to make you humble in order to make this moment possible.[1]

Nevertheless, steeped as we are in the self-esteem ethic of our society, we misread the still, small voice. We misread it because we have misidentified the needs of our heart.

I remember one day going to the exercise room of the condominium complex where we were living in Salt Lake City and meeting a woman whose face and name were unfamiliar. I thought maybe my poor memory was doing me in, but she assured me that it was probably just that we hadn't encountered one another before: "You're probably one of those people who goes to church, and you won't see me there. I don't go. If I go to church, there's always something they talk about that makes me feel less good about myself—and nobody needs that. If I stay home my self-esteem doesn't take a beating, so I stay home."

We, as a society, believe that we must choose things that make us feel good about ourselves (that being our paramount need, in our view). We could call this tendency *striving for pride.* The problem is that the real need of our heart is to be close to our Father in Heaven. That need requires humility, and in striving for pride we are seeking something that is diametrically opposed to humility. As C. S. Lewis so eloquently put it:

> As long as you are proud, you cannot know God. A proud man is always looking down on things and people:

1. C. S. Lewis, *Mere Christianity* (New York: Simon & Schuster, 1996), 114.

> and, of course, as long as you are looking down, you cannot see something that is above you.[2]

Humility is the acknowledged dependence on our Father in Heaven's love that will lead to peace. And peace is our hearts' *actual* yearning. We must look deeply enough into our hearts to identify that real need. My friend from the exercise room did not, I'm sure, eliminate her stress by trying to deny it. She would be better off confronting her imperfection with meekness and getting from her Father in Heaven the peace for which she is yearning.

Each of us, in our human way, yearns for peace yet strives for pride. Because the two qualities are opposites, we are obviously engaging in a self-defeating effort.

Perhaps it would be helpful to identify some of the behaviors that manifest our inner confusion.

The Shortcut Seeker

As I was heading into a conference where I was to do a workshop titled "Feeling Unity with Others and with God," a young woman came up to me and touched my arm.

"I'm so glad you're going to be talking about unity. It's exactly what I need."

"Oh, I think that's what we all need," I said. "When we don't feel at one with others, it leaves a knot in the pit of our stomach."

"It sure does," she said. "It makes me feel so inadequate and lonely."

2. Ibid., 111.

"Unity is a necessary element of peace—that's for sure," I responded.

"I hope you're going to tell us how to get it."

"I will," I promised.

Later I recognized the young woman when she entered the room. I smiled and made mental note. For the better part of forty-five minutes I worked through the scriptures, talking first about the great joys of accepting one another's goals as our own, and the self-sacrifice and long-suffering that may require.

"It is often a matter," I said, "of coming to an understanding about what's important and what is right. Having peace in our soul looms so much larger than our petty individual desires. Peace is the word we use to describe our feelings when we are one with our Father in Heaven. That oneness makes us deeply committed to the righteous goals of our fellows and acquiescent about the things that don't matter. It requires the virtues that the Lord lists in section 107 of the Doctrine and Covenants, verse 30. In this verse the Lord is addressing the presiding quorums of the Church. He is telling them that they must reach agreement on decisions to govern the Church. A feeling of unanimity will be necessary or, the Lord warns, the decisions will not have adequate power. He tells them that to gain access to this power in their decisions—this power that I call oneness with God—their decisions must be made 'in all righteousness, in holiness, and lowliness of heart, meekness and long-suffering, and in faith, and virtue, and knowledge, temperance, patience, godliness, brotherly kindness and charity.'

"This is the list," I concluded. "This is the list of what we must bring to our relationships in order to feel unified with them and with God. The same virtues that the brethren strive for to achieve unanimity in their decisions are the virtues that we must strive for in order to achieve the feeling of unity that will bring us to peace.

"I promised someone in this room that I would tell them how to get unity—and how to feel the peace that comes from it. This is it. This is the list."

The young woman said quickly and with a note of frustration, "Oh, I meant something we can *do!*" We all laughed.

"The problem is," I answered, "if we can't *do* it, we can't *have* it. It's hard for all of us. That's why we must learn to be patient with ourselves. Perfection is not of this world, but we strive continually for those loving virtues and are blessed in our efforts. Ultimately, the promise is that peace will come. It will be a gift from God. No other answer—no shortcut indulging our natural man—will really work."

All of us would like there to be something we could do to achieve perfection by our own standard, under our own power, and in our current state of being. Although it is an illusion, it sounds easier than working toward it step by step. Perfection that we don't quite understand and which requires lifelong progression and a gradual gift of God sounds, at first blush, like pie in the sky. The natural man is not a patient one. We don't want something open-ended. We want something that in our current state of being we can measure, check off, finish, and call enough. As a friend of mine would say, we don't want process, we want outcome. And outcome quickly. But we must learn patience in process if we are ever to achieve peace.

Our real need is indeed for something we can do—but, wanting to feel good about ourselves, we look instead for something we can *be done with.*

Knowing that we are still in process does not bring the pride we think we need, but it does bring a deeply comforting acknowledgment of our dependence on our trustworthy

Father in Heaven. It does bring peace—which is truly our yearning.

THE CHECKLISTER

Not all of us, as we strive for pride, are looking for shortcuts. As a matter of fact, some of us devote our lives to doing everything the instruction book outlines and then consider good feelings our right. And then we are angry when peace does not accompany our accomplishment. We may become exhausted from the effort, and still we do not have a feeling of well-being. We feel we have done our part and have been cheated.

A beautiful sister missionary knocked on our door one day in Montreal and said she wanted to talk with me. I had a particular admiration for her. She worked hard and gave much. We went to an upstairs bedroom to visit, and she kicked off her shoes and put her feet up on one of the beds while I sat up on the other one. Our conversation went something like this:

"Oh, Sister Rasband," she began. "I'm so tired. I'm just exhausted." It was certainly understandable.

"Take a day off," I suggested. "Spend it in bed. Don't allow your health to deteriorate."

It quickly became apparent that I was not understanding at all. "It won't do any good," she said with frustration and anger.

"Sounds like the work is getting tough to do."

"It's not that! It's just that I'm breaking my neck out here. Working unbelievable hours. And I feel like the Lord is never satisfied with my efforts. There's no peace at all!"

"Oh." I was beginning to understand. "Maybe you're not giving the Lord what he wants."

"I'm working seventy hours a week. I'm studying an hour every day. I'm teaching investigators and they're accepting the gospel. I'm keeping perfect records. For crying out loud! *When is it enough?*"

"Perhaps the Lord is not as much of a counter as you are. You need to give him your heart. When he has that, the peace will come."

"How much more of my heart can I give him? I'm practically all used up." She buried her head in the pillow.

I got up and walked around the bed, then leaned down and put an arm around her. I was struggling for a way to explain it.

"The way you're doing things right now, it's as if you're writing huge checks to the Lord from your adequate bank account. He appreciates them and all that. He's putting the money to good use. But what he really wants is the box you keep under your bed. The one with the rock you found at the beach on your favorite day of all time, and that silly safety pin your boyfriend gave you that day he told you he loved you. Until the Lord has that box, it will never be enough. It will never be enough because that box is the symbol that there is something you hold more dear than him. Your need is to give him that box. If and when you can do that, the measuring will stop. You will feel him telling you when it is enough, and the peace will descend."

She understood. "You mean like Abraham?"

"Yes, to a degree, like Abraham."

When Abraham climbed Mt. Moriah, he believed that the Lord would require him to sacrifice his son Isaac there. Abraham loved and trusted the Lord; he had given the Lord his entire heart. So, even though the thought of that demand must have agonized him, Abraham stood ready to meet it. As did Isaac. They climbed all the way to the top of that mount. They were committed to holding nothing back. Only then did the Lord tell them that it was enough. The sacrifice of Abraham's son would not be necessary.

Most of us are not like Abraham. Most of us have something that we would hold back—something that we think is too much for the Lord to ask. We measure; we keep score; we give what anyone ought to see is clearly sufficient. And we feel we need to carefully guard the box under our bed. *We* want to be the ones to say when it is enough. We misidentify our need, and peace eludes us.

Many of us have something in the box that we would withhold from our Father in Heaven. Sort of like saying, "Please, Lord, ask anything but that!" For some it is as small as Sunday football, while for others it is as important as status or peer-group popularity. It may be only that one more hour of our time or that one more dollar of our money. It may be someone on our visiting teaching list or home teaching list that we don't want to visit. Meanwhile, stress builds and peace eludes.

The real need of our hearts is total trust; it is to think in terms of being willing to give whatever is required by our Father in Heaven. We misidentify our need and believe instead that we need for God to be pleased with whatever *we're* willing to give—whatever *we* call "enough." At the Missionary Training Center we often hear that it is asking "just too much" to restrict phone calls home and visits from friends and family, or that the dress code is "dumb," and the schedule "unrealistic." Peace, however, is a gift from God, and we cannot choose the terms on which it is given. Only God can do that. Unless we confront the true need of our hearts, we are apt never to fill it.

Perhaps, for many of us, the hardest things to give up are our sources of self-esteem. Much as we've been taught the principle of delegation, for instance, we don't want to rearrange our work load to spend time with our family, because then someone else would get the sense of accomplishment and the "praise of men" for the project we're completing. Interestingly, it is often family needs for which we feel we've "done enough."

Most often, I think, the treasure we keep guarded in our little box is our patience or our trust. I talked with a young woman recently who had decided to marry a man who she knew would not make a good husband or a good priesthood leader for her and her children. "I've been promised a righteous companion," she told me, "but I'm almost thirty. I've been patient enough."

The exceptional sister missionary who called on me in desperation that day in Montreal confided in me later that what *she* had been guarding was her autonomy. "I called missionary rules 'the order of the white handbook,'" she said, "and it made me angry! I thought it was too many nitpicky little things, and I resented being told what to do."

Whatever is in our box, we want to keep it under our bed. Our control of that box is precious to us. We put the limit of our service just short of our whole heart. We will nearly kill ourselves with checking off what ought to be enough, but yet we still may be withholding the box under the bed, something that represents where our heart is. We may not even be conscious of it. We may guard it without realizing we're doing so. But conscious or not, when we get to the point where we've checked off what we think should be enough, we withdraw, and then we fail to understand the stress that ensues. We might call this practice "checklisting."

The checklister is so common that the Lord has recorded

many examples in the scriptures. One such example is one of the most well known in the New Testament.

A rich young man came to the Lord with questions about what he should do to obtain eternal life (see Mark 10:17–22). I suspect the rich young man was feeling weary in his mind and faint. The Prophet Joseph Smith taught that "such was, and always will be, the situation of the saints of God, that unless they have an actual knowledge that the course they are pursuing is according to the will of God they will grow weary in their minds, and faint." The Prophet further said, "It is through the medium of the sacrifice of all earthly things that men do actually know that they are doing the things that are well pleasing in the sight of God."[3]

Perhaps the rich young man could have as easily phrased his question, "When is it enough?" or "I'm exhausted! When will I have peace?"

The Lord's answer came in three stages and is instructive to all of us. First, the Lord responded to the way the young man had addressed him. His greeting to the Lord had been "Good Master." The Lord responded, "Why callest thou me good? there is none good but one, that is, God." This is a rich statement, clearly designed to teach the young man much about the route to eternal life. First, he is directing the listener's attention to his Father in Heaven and reminding him of his dependence on his Father in Heaven's goodness.

Second, I hear in this statement the same irony that I heard in the Savior's response to Pilate (John 18:37): "Thou sayest that I am a king." I hear the Savior (who has long since announced his messiahship; see Luke 4:21) saying to the rich young man, essentially, "You call me 'good' and don't even

---

3. Joseph Smith Jr., *Lectures on Faith* (Salt Lake City, Deseret Book Co., 1985), 67–69.

realize what you're saying, for I am Jehovah, and it is my goodness that will save you." Had the young man understood, the statement would have been a reminder of his dependence on the Atonement for eternal life. It would have been all the answer he needed.

Third, on a lesser level but equally important, the Savior is reminding the young man that, in mortality, nobody but Christ himself is sinless—which is to say that eternal life is perfection and perfection is not a mortal condition.

Had the young man been listening carefully, that first answer alone would have been enough. It would have told him that he was expecting the impossible; that his own merit would never be enough by itself to give him eternal life. Or, as 2 Nephi 25:23 so eloquently puts it, "We know that it is by grace that we are saved, after all we can do."

Thus, the Savior reminded him, "There is none good but one, that is, God." But the young man did not have ears to hear, so the Lord continued: "Thou knowest the commandments, Do not commit adultery, Do not kill, Do not steal, Do not bear false witness, Defraud not, Honour thy father and mother" (Mark 10:19).

I hear this as the divine equivalent of "keep a-pitchin' in." Be obedient. Be patient. You will grow. You will experience the mighty change.[4] You will have peace. You will have eternal life. Be patient.

But the rich young man did not have ears to hear this either.

"Master, all these have I observed since my youth."

I can't help but hear echoes here of my exceptional sister missionary: I'm working; I'm studying. When is it enough?

---

4. "The Spirit of the Lord Omnipotent . . . has wrought a mighty change in us, or in our hearts" (Mosiah 5:2).

The next verse tells us that the Lord looked at him and loved him before he proceeded. I am familiar with an ache that perhaps incompletely resembles the pain and joy that filled the Savior's heart for this young man—this wonderful, righteous young man who had kept the basic commandments "from his youth" and who still lacked peace (see D&C 59:23). This striving, anxious young man asked for something he could do and wanted something he could be done with. He had checked off his list and was frustrated that peace had not come. His anxiety had driven him now to ask, "When is it enough?"

But the Spirit can communicate with you that it is "enough" only when for you there is no limit. So the Lord gave the young man his individual application of the higher law. He gave him an opportunity to get rid of his checklist. In essence, we could say the Lord asked for the box under the young man's bed—that which the young man held more dear than the Lord, that which represented his heart. In this case, the box was filled with golden treasure, not just a rock and a safety pin. No matter its contents. The box is the same.

"One thing thou lackest: go thy way, sell whatsoever thou hast, and give to the poor, and thou shalt have treasure in heaven: and come, take up the cross, and follow me" (Mark 10:21).

I think the Lord was saying something like "The need of your heart is to trust me. Be willing to give everything." But the young man apparently thought his need was for a final stamp of approval—something he could do and be done with. The scriptures record that the young man went away sorrowing.

We will never know if the young man would have had his riches returned to him—if his very willingness would have been "enough." And in mortality, he never knew, either.

A different kind of example is found in the story of Shadrach, Meschach, and Abednego. The three were told that if they kept the Lord's commandment and refused to worship an idol, they would be thrown into a fiery furnace. But they held nothing back. They trusted. They kept the commandment.

The king renewed his threat to the three and mocked the Lord God of Israel: "Ye shall be cast the same hour into the midst of a burning fiery furnace; and who is that God that shall deliver you out of my hands?" The three expressed their faith that Jehovah was *able* to save them but at the same time expressed their commitment that whether God saved them or not, they would worship only him. Their loyalty to their covenant made them free of Nebuchadnezzar in either event. They were willing to die. But their willingness was enough. Their martyrdom was not required (see Daniel 3).

Shadrach, Meschach, and Abednego will know forever that they gave enough. We can imagine that their peace is complete. The needs of their hearts are fulfilled.

Moroni said it well: "Love God with all your might, mind and strength, then is his grace sufficient for you" (Moro. 10:32).

It sounds so hard to give in a trusting, unmeasured way. And yet it is the measuring that wears us out. I am continuously amazed at how often the words come out: "I'm tired. I'm exhausted." We know from the words of the Prophet Joseph (see the quotation from *Lectures on Faith*) that this, like other consequences of the search for self-esteem, is not a modern phenomenon. It has been ever thus.

It is precisely this exhaustion the Lord is addressing when he says, "Come unto me, all ye that labour and are heavy laden, and I will give you rest. Take my yoke upon you, and learn of me; for I am meek and lowly in heart: and ye shall find rest unto your souls" (Matt. 11:28).

It is obviously a problem of long standing that men and women need something they can do and look for something they can be done with. Neither are we the first to heap on our own backs a weight that is heavier than we can bear in an endless search for a measurable "enough." As long as it is our own yoke and not his yoke, it is difficult and heavy. I think that's why he has given us the golden reassurance, "My yoke is easy, and my burden is light" (Matt. 11:30).

Once I believed that I could give well-being to others with no yoke at all—by telling them that they were wonderful just the way they were. Now I know that it was the equivalent of flattery and that I was trying to give them pride. It must surely have stood in the way of their peace. A yoke is necessary, I know now, but not a heavy "checklister's yoke." It is the light burden and the easy yoke of giving your whole heart—doing all you can and looking to the Lord to make up for your inadequacy, "for I, the Lord, require the hearts of the children of men" (D&C 64:22).

We can have peace. It comes not so much in "outcome" as in "process." It comes through identifying that the need of our heart is grace, and that grace comes when the motivation for our unmeasured doing is founded in love.

Checklisting is valuable for your daily "to do" list. It is helpful in personal goal setting and assessment of your progress—after all, checklists of sorts are part of such things as interviews for obtaining a temple recommend. But as a way to "bind the Lord" (see D&C 82:10) and demand peace, checklisting is worse than useless. It is a barrier to peace because the Lord works on the level of love: "And ye shall seek me, and find me, when ye shall search for me with all your heart" (Jer. 29:13). He alone fully knows our hearts (see D&C

6:16), and so the offering of grace is fully his decision; the binding is something he does to himself, with marvelous integrity and even more marvelous love, when we do what he says: that is, give him our whole might, mind, and strength.

Divine confidence cannot be achieved by seeking it, suggesting it, or acting as if you have it. It can't be bestowed by the praise of men. It can't be accomplished by behavior that is measured or checked off on a list or made simple. In fact, when used as evidence of outcome instead of process, any of these efforts will prove to be barriers to peace and therefore to true confidence. As long as the focus is on the self in any way, peace will elude us.

Self-assessment may be useful and self-development is a necessity. But self-vaunting will be a barrier—and self-indulgence absolutely deadly.

Peace, and therefore confidence, is an affair of the heart.

We would do well to seek, as the apostle Paul did in his prayers for the Ephesians, "that Christ may dwell in your hearts by faith; that ye, being rooted and grounded in love, may be able to comprehend with all saints what is the breadth, and length, and depth, and height; and to know the love of Christ, which passeth knowledge, that ye might be filled with all the fulness of God" (Eph. 3:17–19).

THE FOURTH KEY

Beware of Insatiability and Blame

Let's take a look at two barriers to peace: insatiability and blame. Peace is the gentle precursor of confidence and is indeed a gift of God to mortals who are humbly striving with all their hearts to make a total commitment to him. Anxiety, however, is just as surely a stressful accompaniment to the search for self-esteem. The search, you see, must result in one of two things: either we achieve self-esteem, or we don't. Either way, it is anxiety producing. Insatiability and blame are products of such anxiety, and both are crippling conditions, enemies to real peace.

If we achieve self-esteem, whether it be unconditionally or by measuring our effort so we can "deserve" it, it will never be enough. Our appetite for the self-congratulatory feelings will always be insatiable. All of us must have this "feeling good about ourselves" continually fed. That which we call self-esteem is a high-maintenance condition, and therefore a barrier to peace.

Blaming others is the result of searching for self-esteem and *not* finding it. This condition is also a barrier to peace.

A friend of mine told me recently about an experience she had when she was asked to open a testimony meeting with prayer. She was exceedingly pleased with herself when she sat down. The prayer had been powerful, and she was sure it would be deeply meaningful to all who heard. These good feelings about herself and her "performance," however, far from being enough, spawned a need to have others notice her eloquence. In each testimony she expected to hear mention of the inspiration her prayer had been to the bearer. She listened carefully for it, though she heard little else of the testimonies. At the end of the meeting, not one of the participants had made note of her prayer. She went home with her "self-esteem" bruised, in spite of the fact that she had initially felt very good about herself indeed. The continual feeding had not taken place.

I think of my friend as particularly courageous for sharing this little happening, although no doubt we can all identify with her. Surely we can all remember times when we wished for more praise than was offered. How many times has each of us participated in a meeting and responded to the question "How did it go?" with, "Not very well, I guess. Nobody commented." If our self-esteem is not constantly fed, it quickly becomes malnourished. A continual flow of praise is necessary to maintain it, and we incessantly feel the stress of trying to make certain our good feelings about ourselves will indeed be perpetuated.

All of us are familiar with stories of movie stars and other celebrities who outlive their spot in the public eye and turn to alcoholism or other forms of expression of private agony. Whatever good feelings they had about themselves—whatever "self-esteem" that fame afforded—it did not leave them with calm and wholeness. It left them with greater needs than they would have had had they never achieved such self-gratification.

No, achieving self-esteem will never bring peace. The self-esteem that the world tells us to seek is not the same as the confidence described in Doctrine and Covenants 121, verses 45 and 46:

"Let thy bowels also be full of charity towards all men and to the household of faith, and let virtue garnish thy thoughts unceasingly; then shall thy confidence wax strong in the presence of God; and the doctrine of the priesthood shall distil upon thy soul as the dews from heaven.

"The Holy Ghost shall be thy constant companion, and thy scepter an unchanging scepter of righteousness and truth; and thy dominion shall be an everlasting dominion, and without compulsory means it shall flow unto thee forever and ever."

This is the confidence that is accompanied by peace. It is the feeling of being one with our Father in Heaven that calms us. As the old English proverb says, "The best way to see divine light is to put out your own little candle."[1]

Self-esteem may bring bravado, but not real confidence. And the insatiable nature of self-esteem is an anxiety that makes peace impossible. It is as the prophet Joseph Smith taught: "Such was, and always will be, the situation of the saints of God, that unless they have an actual knowledge that the course they are pursuing is according to the will of God they will grow weary in their minds, and faint."[2]

There is actually an advantage, Alma taught, to being "brought to a lowliness of heart," to being "compelled to be humble." Alma explains: "For a man sometimes, if he is compelled to be humble, seeketh repentance" (or in other words,

---

1. Andy Zubko, ed., *Treasury of Spiritual Wisom* (San Diego: Blue Dove Press, 1996), 119.
2. Joseph Smith Jr., *Lectures on Faith* (Salt Lake City: Deseret Book Co., 1985), 67–68.

puts out his own little candle and lets the Lord's light shine within him).

Some few of those who feel the smallness of their self-esteem do find peace and true confidence precisely because they do not commit to expanding their self-esteem. In other words, when they feel the light of their little candle flickering, they blow it out. We acknowledge that this is not common (few of us identify the need of our hearts that well), but it *is* possible.

We can see an example of both insatiability and blame in the story of Saul, the first king of Israel.

Samuel tells us about Saul's fateful military operation against the Amalekites (see 1 Sam. 15). He had been commanded to utterly destroy *all* of the target people and everything they owned. Nevertheless, he instead spared the king and the best of the animals. The prophet Samuel in reprimanding him reminded him of how his fame and power had been achieved: "When thou wast little in thine own sight, wast thou not made the head of the tribes of Israel and *the Lord* anointed thee king over Israel?" (1 Sam. 15:17; emphasis added).

Samuel reminded Saul that he had been "little" in his own sight. We have no indication that he was looking for self-esteem, only that he didn't have it. The Lord visited him with power and position in his humility. When the incident with the Amalekites occurred, however, Saul was a king and had become, we can assume from his behavior and from Samuel's comment, *large* in his own sight. His self-esteem was insatiable. It needed to be fed. But he made a bad choice, and a prophet of the Lord told Saul that he had done "evil in the sight of the Lord." Saul's self-esteem took a beating. Did he turn to the Lord in humility and repentance the way he did before when he felt "little"? No. He said instead, "But *the people* took of the spoil" (v. 21; emphasis added). This time it appears he was looking for someone to blame.

The difference in the two responses to feeling "little in his own sight" is revealing. Before he was anointed, Saul was compelled to be humble. His personal and family position was poor and he was at the end of an assignment at which he had failed. The Lord could build on that. And he did. The second time, Saul felt important and was searching to feed his insatiable self-image with glory from the victory. When that search didn't work because the prophet reminded him of his weakness, Saul was left with no other way out but finding someone else to blame. Having an unquenchable need for the glory and having it denied by the prophet, Saul could only save his own self-image by passing the buck. It is the inevitable outcome for all of us who focus on ourselves and find the picture not to our liking. If we don't change our focus entirely, we will look for someone to blame.

I see this flaw in my own life so embarrassingly often that I have spent considerable time looking for something slight enough to share here as an example so as not to thwart completely my own striving for pride. As luck would have it, the illustration was provided for me only a few days ago by a new friend.

"Do you think you could sew one of these for us?"

"Uh . . . I'm sorry, but I don't sew at all."

"Really?"

"Well, you see, I wasn't raised to sew. My mother never taught me, and it wasn't offered in the schools when I was young."

"But didn't you just yesterday tell me about your sisters who sew so beautifully?"

"Uh . . ."

"Gotcha!"

She had indeed "got" me. It is obviously my own responsibility that I never learned to sew. How much more intact my peace would have been had I simply acknowledged that fact, with humility, without efforts to defend my self-image. But no—I chose to blame my poor sainted mother, and the public school system. Likely I would have added to the list had I been able to think of anyone else to blame.

Among missionaries this result of a fruitless commitment to self-esteem is particularly common. One especially insightful missionary told me near the end of his mission: "I so wanted to distinguish myself right away when I arrived in the field. It didn't work. So I became anti-leadership. In the first place, I felt like I was looking good by putting them down, and in the second place, I convinced myself that it was the leaders' policies that made it impossible for me to achieve success. After a while it felt crummy to be so negative all the time, so I decided to just accept the fact that I was not going to be so special, and I just started praying for the ability to do the work." He blew out his little candle and went to the Lord for his light.

It should not be surprising to any of us who read the scriptures that this young man's prayers were answered. He was more than able to do the work. He finished his mission as a truly distinguished missionary. He put aside his search for self-esteem, stopped blaming anyone that he didn't have it, acknowledged that he was nothing compared to the Lord, and was therefore willing to simply be used as an instrument in the Lord's hands. Along with the peace that followed, he also experienced glimmers of true confidence—and even the praise of men, though that is not what he was seeking.

The Christian paradox is real and true. Only when we lose ourselves will we find ourselves.

If you are experiencing a continual, insatiable need for

reinforcement of your good feelings about yourself, if you are finding yourself blaming others when you feel bad about yourself, it should be a clue to you that although you are yearning for peace, you are striving for pride. The Lord invites us to abandon our search for self-esteem and instead turn to him with a broken heart and a contrite spirit. When we are little in our own sight, he can make us leaders in Israel.

"Humble yourselves in the sight of the Lord, and he shall lift you up" (James 4:10).

THE FIFTH KEY

Avoid Self-Consciousness

Our Father in Heaven is unconcerned with our current state of competence. He directs us instead to be diligent within it. We need to gain that perspective. In other words, we need to fight our self-consciousness and devote our attention instead to diligent, heart-involved, unmeasured service. Hard as that sounds, it must be our goal.

I remember well when the understanding of this principle was dawning in my awareness. I had read and pondered the multitude of scriptures that direct us to see our nothingness, to be humble, to have a broken heart and a contrite spirit. I had already come to understand that there was pressure and stress in searching for self-esteem. I began to believe that the way out of the insatiability/blame trap was to switch from a positive pressure to a negative one. For a while I believed that we should focus on our understanding that the natural man is an enemy to God—a sort of self-imposed, forced humility. I struggled with that concept, though, because I observed that such a negative view only fostered self-pity and was an equal pressure. It was like changing deck chairs on the Titanic. Both attitudes were doomed to failure. Both were characterized by intense self-consciousness. Peace was in neither.

One day, still struggling, I thought about Moses and Enoch. They were among those, after all, from whom I had taken what I had perceived to be a focus on the negative. Suddenly, joyfully, I saw the answer. It was to be found in the Lord's response to their anguish—not in the anguish itself.

Moses' experience on the Mount included this profound discovery: "And as he was left unto himself, he fell unto the earth . . . and he said unto himself: Now, for this cause I know that man is nothing, which thing I never had supposed" (Moses 1:9–10).

After seeing "the world and the ends thereof, and all the children of men," Moses was buffeted by Satan's temptations, and then "Moses began to fear exceedingly; and as he began to fear, he saw the bitterness of hell. Nevertheless, calling upon God, he received strength" (v. 20).

Later in the book of Moses we find an account of God's revealing himself to Enoch: "And when Enoch had heard these words, he bowed himself to the earth, before the Lord, and spake . . . , saying: Why is it that I have found favor in thy sight, and am but a lad, and all the people hate me; for I am slow of speech; wherefore am I thy servant?

"And the Lord said unto Enoch: Go forth and do as I have commanded thee" (Moses 6:31–32).

It's enlightening to compare the Lord's response with what our own might be. The Lord did not reassure with, "Oh, nonsense! You're terrific." That would be our way. Neither, however, did he say, "How right you are, you really are dreadful," which was what I had been perceiving as an antidote. Instead, he simply *ignored* their state of adequacy. He didn't indulge them in their self-focus at all. He expected

Moses and Enoch to get their strength from the Lord, and he told them simply to keep his commandments.

It seems to me that in these stories the Lord is revealing to all of us that it is counterproductive for him to indulge us in our self-consciousness. He is saying to all of us simply: Go forth and do as I have commanded you. Call upon God and receive your strength.

The call to be a prophet must be awesomely humbling. Scripture records some instances of the Lord's responses to prophets who fear to serve due to their focus on their inadequacy. For example, Jeremiah, when he received his call, responded with, "Ah, Lord God! behold, I cannot speak: for I am a child." The Lord told him not to say that, "for thou shalt go to all that I shall send thee . . . for I am with thee to deliver thee" (Jer. 1:6–8). Or in other words, call upon God to receive your strength; go forth and do as I have commanded you.

Another prophet, Isaiah, responded to his call with "Woe is me! For I am undone; because I am a man of unclean lips, and I dwell in the midst of a people of unclean lips." The Lord answered: "Thine iniquity is taken away, and thy sin purged." He then expressed his need for a servant and Isaiah, apparently relieved of his self-focus, said, "Here am I. Send me" (Isa. 6:5, 7–8).

Abraham, like Moses, fell on his face in abject humility when he was first given the blessing of the covenant. When I read Genesis 17, my mind fills with what I would like to say to Abraham in reassurance: "Oh, Abraham! If anybody deserves it, it is you. You have been noble and obedient and righteous against all odds. Abraham, you're wonderful." But that was not the Lord's response—no encouragement of self-focus here. He told him, "A father of many nations *have I made thee*" (v. 5; emphasis added). And in verse 9: "Thou shalt keep my covenant therefore, thou, and thy seed after thee in their generations." Or in other words, get your strength from me and keep my commandments.

Listen, then, to the peace that Abraham experienced. It is beautifully expressed in his words, which I quote from the Pearl of Great Price: "Therefore, eternity was our covering, and our rock and our salvation" (Abr. 2:16).

There are many scriptural instances of the Lord's refocusing response to man's self-consciousness, and I have found not one scriptural example of the Lord's indulging man in his self-focus with the kind of reassuring praise that most of us would offer.

It has become clear to me that the enemy to our peace is self-consciousness itself. Further, it became clear that the escape from self-consciousness is through the doorway of repentance and forgiveness, not reassurance and ego protection, "for a man sometimes, if he is compelled to be humble, seeketh repentance; and now surely, whosoever repenteth shall find mercy; and he that findeth mercy and endureth to the end the same shall be saved" (Alma 32:13).

Peace is not in self-esteem or even in self-awareness at all. Peace is in mercy. Peace is in calling upon God to receive our strength and keeping the commandments. Peace is in enduring to the end. Peace is diametrically opposed to self-focus.

It was much later that I noticed another paragraph in C. S. Lewis' *Mere Christianity* that reminded me that I was not the first to struggle with this concept and come up with a similar answer:

"The real test of being in the presence of God is that you either forget about yourself altogether or see yourself as a small dirty object. It is better to forget about yourself altogether."[1]

Much better.

Like a new word that you hear everywhere once you are

---

1. C. S. Lewis, *Mere Christianity* (New York: Simon & Schuster, 1996), 112.

introduced to it, the truth about self-esteem now seems to me to be present in every story, every principle of the gospel.

President Gordon B. Hinckley tells the story of a letter that he received from his father when he was on his mission. The young prophet-to-be was discouraged. He wrote to his father that he wasn't getting anywhere with his missionary work in the British Isles. He couldn't see any point in wasting his time and his father's money. The letter he received in return was short and to the point: "Dear Gordon, I have your recent letter. I have only one suggestion: forget yourself and go to work." Later, President Hinckley would say, "That July day in 1933 was my day of decision. A new light came into my life and a new joy into my heart. The fog of England seemed to lift, and I saw the sunlight. Everything good that has happened to me since then I can trace back to the decision I made that day."[2]

I wonder if President Hinckley's father had been reading about Jeremiah, Enoch, Moses, or Isaiah. Or was he so closely in tune with his Father in Heaven that he intuitively knew how an earthly parent should respond? In any event, the effect on his righteous son was the same: obedience, followed by success in the mission field.

Perhaps a homely little allegory will help you bring to mind why self-consciousness is an enemy and how it damns us.

Someone on the Corner

Let's say there is a garden you would like to visit. There is a meeting there of people whom you hold most dear. The

---

2. As quoted in Sheri L. Dew, *Go Forward with Faith: The Biography of Gordon B. Hinckley* (Salt Lake City: Deseret Book Co., 1996), 64.

garden, however, is behind a gate in the middle of a large city, and you must find a parking place for the vehicle you're driving. There are no time constraints. You have all day, as it were, but you deeply want to get there eventually, and so you circle around and around looking for a place to park. In all the city there is only one space. It is right in front of the gate to the garden, but it is just a mite small. At first you think you'll never make it, but it is either park in that space or not at all, so you remind yourself that there are no clocks in the garden, and you decide that with time and effort you can make it. You begin. You line up and turn your wheels, but find that you are crooked and too far out; so you pull out and try again. It keeps happening. Nevertheless, with each failure you get a little closer, and since you have no pressure of time, you keep trying. It is a minor frustration that it takes so many tries, but you keep at it and lose count of the failures.

Now let's change the scenario a bit. Let's say you notice someone on the corner watching. Suddenly the frustration is agonizing when you fail. You may even be less efficient in the next try and end up farther out instead of closer. Eventually, if that someone continues to watch, you may become so exasperated that you will pull out entirely and stop trying. Even though you desperately wanted to go into the garden, it begins to be not worth it.

The pressure increases if that someone is verbally evaluating you from the vantage point—whether in honesty or flattery, praise or derision. Honest praise, of course, feels a bit better, but the level of pressure created by consciousness of the observer will not decrease in any case. The pressure to come into the parking place perfectly, whether to make the praise valid or to disprove the ridicule, becomes so intense that failures become impossible to bear. You have allowed the observer to make it absolutely impossible to keep your thoughts on the joys that await you in the garden.

When we are conscious of someone on the corner, it is indeed fear that stops our progress, and as John expresses it so well in 1 John 4:18: "Fear hath torment." There is only one way to escape that torment: identify the someone-on-the-corner. Deal with him.

It is not God. Figuratively speaking, the Holy Ghost sits next to us in the car and gently directs us. He is not relentless but merciful. One of the Spirit's names, after all, is the Comforter. He would remind us continually, not of our parking job, but of the joys that await in the garden.

The someone-on-the-corner may be our fellowman, but if it is, it is only because we have invited him there—we have highly regarded his view. So our peers are not really to blame.

The truth is that each of us is our own damning observer. Even though we must leave our quest in order to stand on the corner and observe ourselves, we still do it. Even though the pressure of observing our parking talent or lack of it is filling us with agony, we still do it. Even though the Spirit is telling us that mercy is available, and that we should therefore "forget ourselves and go to work," we still stand on the corner and observe ourselves. We need to get back in the car, get rid of our self-consciousness, and keep trying.

The righteous evaluation that we need in order to straighten up and get into the parking place can be done from the driver's seat with the help of the Spirit. That kind of personal assessment can be a great servant. But when we stand on the corner and praise or deride ourselves, or highly regard the praise or derision of others, evaluation becomes the master. And it is a poor master.

The human tendency to approach a goal with self-awareness as both method and motivation is a pressure that I don't believe our Father in Heaven would ever put upon us. Our Father's way would be to remove our stress by refocusing us on the garden, extending his mercy and his direction. We gain access to his guidance through listening to the still, small voice and loving the Lord with all our heart, might, mind, and strength. The result of our obedience is that for which we truly yearn: peace.

"Awake my soul! No longer droop in sin. Rejoice, O my heart, and give place no more for the enemy of my soul" (2 Ne. 4:28).

PART 2

The Keys to Commitment

"He that loveth not knoweth not God; for God is love."

—1 John 4:8

THE SIXTH KEY

Love and Help Others

While once I put decorated badges on young people saying "I am lovable and capable," I have now evolved into a person who would want those badges to read "I am loved and grateful." Feeling loved and grateful is the route to peace, whereas focusing on whether or not we are lovable and capable only fans the flame of self-consciousness.

Love Is the Great Energy Source

When one of our sons was in the first grade, the teacher encouraged the students to use their fledgling writing skills by assigning them to write a one-sentence paper. "Write down," she directed, "what you would like to be instead of yourself." She hoped to receive papers from children who might want to be lions, tigers, or maybe fire engines. She wanted, she told me later, to explore the children's dreams of power and service.

Our son, who was normally a cooperative student, turned in a blank sheet of paper. When asked the reason, he replied,

"I'm sorry, Miss Osborne, I really tried. I thought and thought the whole time, but I couldn't think of anything I'd rather be than me."

I was, of course, pleased to receive this report from his teacher at conference time. One surely wants one's child to be content and secure.

I am aware that it is fashionable to evaluate our son's feeling by saying that our child loved himself. While that assessment is certainly meant to be complimentary, I believe that calling it love of self is a misnomer and that that mislabeling has become not only a semantic error but a serious invitation to self-consciousness—an invitation that more often than not is accepted in our society. I believe that such feelings as our son expressed are indeed the *result* of love, but not directly an *act* of love.

This child's thought was much the same as that of Shakespeare when he wrote Sonnet Number 29.[1] In the early part of the piece Shakespeare describes his feelings when he is depressed and full of self-loathing—how he wishes he were someone else with all their advantages and gifts. He even tries

---

1. When in disgrace with fortune and men's eyes
I all alone beweep my outcast state,
And trouble deaf Heaven with my bootless cries,
And look upon myself and curse my fate,
Wishing me like to one more rich in hope,
Featured like him, like him with friends possessed,
Desiring this man's art and that man's scope,
With what I most enjoy contented least—
Yet in these thoughts myself almost despising,
Haply I think on thee, and then my state,
Like to the lark at break of day arising
From sullen earth, sings hymns at Heaven's gate,
For thy sweet love remembered such wealth brings
That then I scorn to change my state with kings.

to pray and finds that his self-consciousness, his intensely painful self-awareness, stops him from connecting with God. Then he thinks of someone who loves him, and the thought of that love warms him and changes his feelings completely:

> For thy sweet love remembered such wealth brings
> That then I scorn to change my state with kings.

Perhaps in our stumbling way my husband and I were able to give our son enough love to make him scorn to change his state with lions and tigers; or perhaps he had an innate way of receiving love directly from his Father in Heaven. One way or another, he felt loved. And being loved made it possible for him to have delight in being himself. I believe that his feelings of security were nothing more or less than gratitude for being loved and for the gifts of God that make up his particular set of resources—a childish expression of the beautiful truth expressed in scripture: "Every good gift and every perfect gift is from above, and cometh down from the Father of lights" (James 1:17).

The conventional wisdom is that the reason love works is that when we are loved, we learn that we are lovable. I believe that the conventional wisdom is wrong. I believe that (like Moses, Enoch, Jeremiah, and Isaiah) when we are loved, we learn that to the person who loves us, *it doesn't matter whether we are lovable or not.* Our behavior may hurt and disappoint; consequences will have to be paid. Nevertheless, the source of love—our security base—is utterly dependable, notwithstanding our weakness. When our lovability doesn't matter, when we know we will be loved in success or failure, in delight or sorrow, we become free to stop focusing on ourselves at all; we are relieved of the stress of self-consciousness, and we are energized to risk giving our hearts to those deeds that will bring peace. I am describing the committed love that a husband and wife promise one another at the altar: for better or for worse, in sickness or in health. It is the security of an utter gift of commitment from those who love us. If the love is real, we are free to have the comfort of being ourselves. It is a launching pad from which we can risk in order to achieve. Not all people have it available from an earthly source. Not all people who have it available benefit from it. But it is the source of energy.

Our son was not stating that he was lovable enough as he was. He was stating that he could do anything he wanted to do as himself. He knew he was loved and so it simply didn't matter. He was willing to risk using the power that was in him.

It is the nature of language that several concepts can share one word, and that is certainly true with the word *love.* It has many meanings. When Paul told us that "God loveth a cheerful giver" (2 Cor. 9:7), for instance, he was talking about the love that is a reaction to something. That use of the word indicates that one is extremely pleased with whatever it is that one is responding to. It is human to want to evoke a response. Our experience is, therefore, that someone's pleasurable reaction to us may be a motivator. It is not, however, an energizer, because with a desire for response as motivation, the risk of *not* pleasing is what looms largest. That is anxiety producing. We are only truly, righteously energized by being freed of self-consciousness.

The love that we talk of when we are yearning for peace, the love that energizes and empowers another human being by giving a base of security, is the kind of love John was talking about when he said, "For God so loved the world, that he gave his only begotten Son" (John 3:16). That gift of love is a gift given freely to all—unconditional physical redemption from the Fall coupled with the opportunity to seek spiritual redemption as well. No matter to what unlovable depths we allow ourselves to sink, God's loving hand is still extended to us, with the invitation to repent and come unto him. This loving invitation is withheld only in the most extreme circumstances. And even those extreme circumstances we know in advance how to avoid. His love is completely reliable. Because his love is constant and dependable—because we can rely upon its always being there—we can forget ourselves and get to work. Our efforts can be directed to showing him we return his love instead of trying to get him to love us. He already loves us. It comes out of his divine heart—not out of our lovability.

The kind of love, however tender, that is a response, that is based on another's lovability, may be only admiration. Admiration brings with it the stress of self-consciousness. When we get our security from being admired, we learn that we must continue to be seen as admirable in order to feel secure. We have no control over the caprice of another's perception, so our foundation feels shaky. Our whole attention has to be directed to our self's survival. It's a barrier to peace.

I was tending my grandson recently, a favorite activity of mine, and I picked him up from preschool. He was wearing a yellow crown emblazoned with big blue letters: "I AM SPECIAL." I thought at once about the badges I had put on the coats of my youth conference attendees. I thought about our missionary who reached the point of not trying to be "special" anymore. I thought about how I would love to have relieved my precious grandson of the pressure to be special. How much better it would have been if the crown had said, "I AM SPECIAL TO MY TEACHER." He would then have known that he was valued without condition, without burden. It is such a small difference in semantics, but such a large difference in comfort. It changes how we receive the expressions of love from others, and it changes how we give expressions of love as well.

Energizing, empowering, security-giving love comes out

of the lover. We love not because someone is lovable but because we are able to love.

Sometimes, not separating the meanings of the word *love,* we work at finding people's lovable qualities and try to concentrate on them so that we can, as we believe, learn to love them in a security-giving way. When we do that, however, we are not really working at *loving* in the way that we have been commanded, but at admiring. The commandment is to *love* one another "as I have loved you." I am confident that it means the way the Lord has loved *all of us*—not just the cheerful givers, though he wants us all to be that; not just those who obey, though he wants us all to do that. He is not commanding us to *admire* one another, but to be there for one another, as he is there for us—love always at the ready. The love must come out of our hearts, not out of our reaction. If we could not love on command, the Lord would not have commanded us to love.

When we love without the necessity for others to be lovable, we will *see* their virtues, not look for them. What's more, the list of virtues will grow, because we will be giving them the security from which they can risk proving the Lord's promise: "But he that doeth truth cometh to the light"(John 3:21).

Or in other words, he that *does* obey or he that *is* a cheerful giver gains access to the love that has always been there—available and constant.

I remember once, many years ago, walking with a friend to Sunday School class as she criticized a speaker who had just concluded his remarks.

"I just hate it when people say that!"

"What?" I asked.

"Oh, that business about 'I love every one of you.' He doesn't even *know* every one of us. It's just a show. I've never even met him."

"Hmmm," I answered. "Don't you think you can love people you don't know? Or even people who aren't lovable?"

"No, of course not!"

"I think you can. I think the kind of love he was talking about is an action, not a reaction. I think he feels so full of love this morning that nothing he could know about us would stop him from loving us."

"Well," she said, "I'd have to think about that. When I love somebody it's because I've got to know them and found them lovable."

"Yeah," I answered, "I think most of us do that most of the time. But there are times when I'm so grateful for being loved, or so keyed in to God's love for me, that I really have it pouring out to everyone. And I think there are even some people, like my children, for instance, for whom I'm so grateful that I have love for them all the time. Anyway, I know that my love for others comes out of me—not them."

A few years later my friend was leaving the ward. She stood at the pulpit and said, "I can't bear to leave. I love every one of you. If you're like I used to be, you don't really believe that, because some of you I don't know well at all. But I *do* love you. I am so full of love for you that nothing I could know about you would change my mind. There are also people in this ward whom I admire. But I love you whether or not I have had the opportunity to find out what I can admire in you. I thank my Heavenly Father for giving you to me to love."

Imagine what might have been her farewell address with her previous mind-set. And let's all admit that at times we have felt the way she might have felt at one time: "I love this ward because so many of you are professionals. You have great musical talent here, and your Sunday School teachers are marvelous scriptorians. Many of you are charitable people and brought food in to me when I had my baby. Some of you are so friendly; you smile at me every week. I wish I had known more of you, because I'm sure there are more people here I could love as well."

With this approach, many of the ward members would have a moment of pride. It would feel very good indeed in the short range to those who were professionals, musicians, or scriptorians. Those who had brought in food would have felt a nod inside that they too had been acknowledged, and those who always smiled would also have felt temporary self-satisfaction. What of those who were not included in the groups she mentioned? What pain of guilt or inadequacy?

For all, there would have been some pressure in the long range, some condition on their security. If I am "loved" because I have great musical talent, for instance, how do I feel if I make a mistake in my performance? Might it lessen my desire to risk performing again, or perhaps pressure me to perform well again to feed my insatiable need for recognition?

With the farewell address this good friend gave, however, everyone felt the love of their Heavenly Father. *Everyone* could go home feeling that they wanted to learn to love in the same way that had brought her such joy. Everyone could feel a connection to her, a true sisterhood or brotherhood, that allowed them to forget themselves and feel love for her and for God. All were energized by her love to risk loving others themselves.

That's what nonreactive, unconditional love does. It energizes. It empowers. It eliminates the fear of risk, the fear of doing, as when Isaiah, by the Lord's mercy, was given the strength to say "Here am I; send me" (Isa. 6:8). Unconditional love eliminates the insatiable need for recognition. It makes it possible to get one's strength from the Lord and to keep the commandments: "Perfect love casteth out fear: because fear hath torment" (1 Jn. 4:18).

We have all heard people give talks like the one my friend might have given. Most of us have even given them ourselves in one way or another. My own past is littered with such speeches. I once honestly believed that admiration was peace giving. But it is the love that comes out of the giver that is the great source of energy.

That feeling our son had in his first grade class has been rightly sought after because it leads to peace. What a shame that it has been mislabeled as self-esteem, because that has sent the search in a direction diametrically opposed to the goal. It has sent us striving for pride. Oh, how many people would be so much happier if that kind of confidence had been identified as the gratitude it was, and people had made their search for that.

The lucky among us have received enough pure affection from parents and family that we feel our gratitude without having to search for it. Nevertheless, even for those who do not have the advantage of a loving family, love is available. There is a folk story that lends understanding and is probably familiar to you. I paraphrase it here to remind you of the truth of the principle it teaches.

A young man died, and upon arrival at the Pearly Gates was treated to a tour of heaven and hell before his final assignment. Hell was first, and he was surprised to find it a room of lavish banquet tables, laden with wonderful things to eat. The people there, however, were emaciated and crying out in hunger. The only way to gain access to the food was with extremely long-handled spoons permanently attached to their hands. When they tried to put the spoons to their mouths, they found it impossible to reach. So the residents of this home of the damned cried out in anguish as well as hunger. The young man on the tour averted his eyes in horror. To see these people starving in the midst of plenty was more than he could bear. He begged to be taken away from this place.

Imagine the young man's surprise on arrival in heaven when he saw identical tables and identical food. The people here, however, were well fed and happy. There was laughter and music and delight. At first the young man thought that the access to the food must be easier. Then he saw it. The food had to be eaten with the same long-handled spoons. The people in heaven, however, had discovered that the long-handled spoons worked very well to feed the food to each other.

Energizing love is served with a long-handled spoon. You *cannot* feed it to yourself. Most of the people in the world believe that you can. They tell you that you must. It becomes an urgency to "feel good about yourself," a strain to admire yourself, a demand to be admirable. The self-focus will keep you from peace.

If you feel hungry for love, grab hold of a long-handled spoon and feed love to others. Miraculously, you will begin to feel love coming directly from your Father in Heaven, which is the purest sort. His long-handled spoon will reach out to you. Lehi said that the love of God was the whitest and the purest and the most delicious of fruits. He said also that you reach it by hanging onto an iron rod (see 1 Ne. 8). That iron rod is the word of God (see 1 Ne. 11:25). The tree is always there, always available, but we cannot find it without the directions found in the word of God, and those directions tell us to feed others, to lose ourselves, abase ourselves, humble ourselves. Love is what makes it possible.

"Let thy bowels also be full of charity towards all men, . . . and let virtue garnish thy thoughts unceasingly; *then* shall thy confidence wax strong" (D&C 121:45; emphasis added).

THE SEVENTH KEY

Gratitude Is Fundamental

The Lord has told us that if we love him we will keep his commandments and we will feed his sheep. John explained that "we love him, because he first loved us" (1 Jn. 4:19).

We have talked about love as the great source of energy, and these scriptural statements would certainly support that. But wait. He first loved *everyone.* Clearly everyone does not love him. If everyone loved him, everyone would focus on keeping the commandments and feeding his sheep. No one would be a judgmental observer of himself or of others. But that utopian state is not the case. All of us experience the demands of self-consciousness to some degree, and some of us are so deeply burdened by self-focus that we are crippled by it. Why do some love him and therefore seek to know and do his will, and some of us simply have become as Paul describes, lovers of our own selves (see 2 Tim. 3:1–2)? What is the difference?

I think we can probably best understand from our perspective as mortal parents and children. Most parents love their children keenly and deeply, yet at times the children do not feel it, despite the parents' best efforts to express it. Knowing their human weaknesses, parents tend to blame themselves for the fact that their love is not reaching the children, and sometimes the children are all too quick to place blame as well.

It is true that earthly parental love is sometimes inadequate, sometimes poorly expressed. However, for the most part, we simply do not see the "love delivery" system clearly. The parents' underdeveloped ability to express love is not the only barrier that stops the love from getting through to the child. The child himself must collect the love that is there for him.

In contrast to earthly parents, our Father in Heaven does not have our human weakness in his ability to love or in his expression. He loves purely and fully. As John says, "God *is* love" (1 Jn. 4:16; emphasis added). Still we fail to collect his love much of the time. We fail to collect it because we have in mind a specific way in which we want the love expressed. If we don't get it *our* way, we refuse to accept it as love. God is perfect, but I'm afraid we are often ungrateful, spoiled children in terms of our collection of his perfect love.

I attended a seminar a few years ago where a questionnaire led us to a conclusion about the expressions of love that we accept. Some of us accept and recognize love when it is expressed verbally, some when another labors in our behalf, some when a loved one offers demonstrative affection, and some when material gifts are given to us. There were still other ways. The series of questions helped us to examine our behavior to see how we are willing to receive love. The director of the seminar suggested that each of us has the right to receive love in the way that we recognize it and accept it. His goal, he said, was that we would use this self-revelation to tell our partners how they should give love to us.

At the end of the quiz I'm sure that I was not alone in feeling more self pity than self-discovery. No one ever gets all they want from others.

I would agree that when we truly love someone we search for righteous ways to show that love. Certainly that should be our response to how God wants us to show our love to him—if for no other reason than that his commands are *always* for our best good.

But keep in mind, the questionnaire was filled out from our point of view as recipient—designed to uncover how we're willing to *receive* love, not how we're willing to give it. Unfortunately, that is typically our focus: what we're getting, not what we're giving (rights versus responsibilities). Because our focus is on how we *receive* love, we come to expect it to be given our way, and refuse to accept it in the way that it is bestowed.

How valuable it would be to our mental health to examine the ways that others *give* love to us instead of the ways we are willing to accept it. Inasmuch as we have a great need to be loved—indeed, a survival need—it seems to me that the great benefit would be in recognizing love that comes to us in ways that are perhaps not our way at all.

God's love is perfect, but we are not. Things of the world which we ignorantly would prefer as an expression of love may not be for our best good. They may even be destructive and therefore would not be an expression of love at all. We must be so humble that we trust the way our perfect Father in Heaven expresses his love for us and be grateful for it without condition. If we don't do that, if we are unwilling to receive it, we fail to collect it. Unrecognized and therefore uncollected, the love does not strengthen us, does not energize us, does not bless us.

God's love—God's wonderful, flawless, encouraging

love—goes largely uncollected. Most of us, like spoiled children, want to dictate the way that he would give it to us. "A loving God," the argument begins, "would surely __________." Fill in the blank any way you wish. For many it is filled in with "would surely not allow children to starve in Ethiopia." For some it is "A loving God would surely not create a child molester."

Interestingly, these blanks are often filled in such a way as to *blame* God for all those things that are not of God at all. God, of course, did not create a child molester. He did, however, allow a child molester to develop and to hurt others. We want only to accept love from someone who manages everything for our comfort, instead of someone who allows agency for our long-term growth. God allows these things and then provides an atonement: "These things I have spoken unto you, that in me ye might have peace. In the world ye shall have tribulation: but be of good cheer; I have overcome the world" (John 16:33).

I have heard the same formula repeated many times: "A loving God would surely see that all of his children were equal in comfort." "A loving God would see that all his children were treated fairly." However the complaint ends, it is the same: man telling God how to love him instead of seeing God's love in God's omniscient expression of it and being grateful.

Gratitude is the key to collecting God's love. When we see the ugliness in the world, we need to be grateful that God has provided a way to overcome it. We need to be grateful for commandments that show us the way through the minefield that is "the world." We need to be grateful for the plan that ultimately redeems us from life's injustices, grateful for life itself (whether or not we understand it). Most of all, we need to be grateful that all of this was accomplished with ultimate and willing sacrifice. All of these things God has given to us not because we are deserving, not because we are important in and of ourselves—but because we are important *to him.* We are his work and his glory (see Moses 1:39). The Lord told Oliver Cowdery to "remember, " and we must remember, too, that "the worth of souls is great in the sight of God" (D&C 18:10). "For God so loved the world, that he gave his only begotten son," and Christ himself "so loved the world that he gave his own life" (John 3:16; D&C 34:3). Such incredible love coming to us from two perfect beings, when we "cannot say that [we] are even as much as the dust of the earth," should be the cause of our inestimable gratitude (Mosiah 2:25). Without that gratitude, we won't collect the love, and without feeling his love we will be handicapped by fear and hopeless doubt. Healing, energizing love is available to all. To collect it, we have only to be grateful enough to give our heart to obedience. For our own peace, "O, how [we] ought to thank [our] heavenly King!" (Mosiah 2:19).

As I see it, this is the order of things: gratitude for God's love leads us to indeed love *him* (see 1 Jn. 4:19). Love for him fills our heart so that he truly has possession of our heart. Giving the heart is giving *whatever* is in the box under the bed. Giving ourselves to God without holding anything back leads to ridding ourselves of self-consciousness. Peace follows.

When we are the giver instead of just the receiver of our Heavenly Father's love, we begin to search for the ways that he would have us love him. The small beginnings come in small ways. All growth is incremental. We start to keep the fundamental commandments simply because he has asked us to. We find the iron rod. Grasping it, we move toward a fulness of the love of God. We get there through humility—humility that is grounded in our deep, self-abasing gratitude. How thrilling that the scriptures do not limit the tree of life from Lehi's dream to just the love of God for us; the scriptural wording can mean our love for him, and our ability to feel his love for others as well. All of these things are pure, white fruit. Oh, what a feast of peace we start toward when first we feel grateful that God loved us so he sent his Son.

Gratitude is the key to giving our whole heart. And the grateful, obedient heart is where we will feel our peace. Not in perfect performance, although our performance will greatly improve; not in a sense of self, although our confidence will be a byproduct; but in humble, indebted understanding that God is mightier than all the earth and that he is our resource, our succor, our security (see 1 Ne. 4:1).

My understanding of the importance of gratitude has come slowly and gradually, as I have had experiences with the spirit of both gratitude and ingratitude in my own disposition. I have learned that it is impossible for me to be happy without feeling grateful, or to feel grateful without being happy. I have noted also that self-awareness is a huge hindrance to gratitude. When my mind and focus are filled with thoughts of myself, I find that I do not notice other things, other good things, for which I should be grateful. And vice versa.

In recent years I have come to view scriptural passages about sign seeking from a new vantage point. I think the reason it is a wicked generation that seeks after a sign is that a righteous one (a grateful one) readily sees the signs all around it. When we are grateful for God's love, counting our blessings becomes something we do because we *see* them, not because we *are looking* to see if there are any. If we do not see the blessings in our life, we are denying the gift and power of God (see Moro. 10:8). I have even wondered: Perhaps, if we deny these blessings, will he one day say to us that we have had blessings enough?

The act of discounting our Heavenly Father's expressions

of love for us and seeking for something that meets our burden of proof regarding his love is ingratitude at the core. That is why it is often said that gratitude is an attitude. For the ungrateful, there is great effort to see their blessings through the fog of self-pity. For the grateful, the vision is in the contentment. It is a perspective, not a checklist. It is the perspective of seeing God instead of ourselves as the source of our strength and our delight. It is the viewpoint of deeply humble and grateful worship. Self-focus interferes with our worship. It encourages us to see if our desires are met instead of being overwhelmed by the love that is being offered in ways we sometimes do not understand. Self-consciousness is the perspective of gratification instead of gratitude. I love the way Annie Dillard expresses it in her book *Pilgrim at Tinker Creek:*

> Self-consciousness [hinders] the experience of the present. It is the one instrument that unplugs all the rest. So long as I lose myself in a tree, say, I can scent its leafy breath or estimate its board feet of lumber. . . . But the second I become aware of myself at any of these activities—looking over my own shoulder as it were—the tree vanishes, . . . as if it had never grown. And time, which had flowed down into the tree bearing new revelations like floating leaves at every moment, ceases.
>
> It is ironic that the one thing that all religions recognize as separating us from our creator—our very self-consciousness—is also the one thing that divides us from our fellow creatures, . . . cutting us off at both ends.[1]

I share Dillard's interest in the irony of self-consciousness. Perhaps, the most ironic fact of all is that when we are truly and fully grateful, we also see those personal gifts that God has

1. Annie Dillard, *Pilgrim at Tinker Creek* (New York: Harper & Row, 1986), 81, 79.

given us. We see the good in ourselves because it would be ungrateful not to see it. It is an awareness that is associated with God, however, and not with ourselves. It is gratitude and worship. It is peace, not pride.

If you would lift the burden of blame and insatiability, learn the secret of gratitude for our worth to both God the Father and God the Son. It is, unfortunately, a well-kept secret. It is not found out in the philosophies of men. It can't start until we are humble, and it can't reach its fulness until we hold fast to the iron rod.

Consider these two scriptural celebrations of the love our Father has for us:

"Nor height, nor depth, nor any other creature, shall be able to separate us from the love of God, which is in Christ Jesus our Lord" (Rom. 8:39).

"Although the fig tree shall not blossom, neither shall fruit be in the vines; the labour of the olive shall fail, and the fields shall yield no meat; the flock shall be cut off from the fold, and there shall be no herd in the stalls:

"Yet I will rejoice in the Lord, I will joy in the God of my salvation" (Hab. 3:17–18).

PART 3

The Keys of Caution

"The philosophies of men, mingled with scripture, soon replace the pure word as it was once written in the holy record. . . . There is no salvation in the teachings or philosophies of men."

—Bruce R. McConkie, *The Millennial Messiah* (Salt Lake City: Deseret Book Co., 1982), 163, 40.

THE EIGHTH KEY

Avoid Mingling Scripture with Worldly Philosophy

It is time now to talk of the scripture that is most often mingled with the philosophies of men that call for self-awareness.

> Then one of them, which was a lawyer, asked him a question, tempting him, and saying,
>
> Master, which is the great commandment in the law?
>
> Jesus said unto him, Thou shalt love the Lord thy God with all thy heart, and with all thy soul, and with all thy mind.
>
> This is the first and great commandment.
>
> And the second is like unto it, Thou shalt love thy neighbour as thyself.
>
> On these two commandments hang all the law and the prophets. (Matt. 22:35–40)

It is common for us to read this scripture as if it actually contains three commandments:

- Love God
- Love your neighbor
- Love yourself

As I have studied this summary of the Law that the Savior gives us, I have come to realize that it contains only two commandments. He introduces the second half of the admonition as "the second" and in the next verse summarizes by referring to "these two commandments."

The first great commandment is to love the Lord our God. Included with the dictum is the instruction as to *how* to love him: with all our heart, soul, and mind. Next comes the second great summary commandment: to love our neighbor. Once again the Lord includes the how-to: as we love ourselves. He could have as easily added the clarification of Paul when the apostle told men to love their wives as themselves, "for no man ever yet hated his own flesh; but nourisheth and cherisheth it" (Eph. 5:29; see vv. 28–33).

Or again when Paul clarified the two great commandments for the Romans, he taught, "And if there be any other commandment, it is briefly comprehended in this saying, namely, Thou shalt love thy neighbour as thyself. Love worketh no ill to his neighbour: therefore love is the fulfilling of the law" (Rom. 13:9–10).

The Savior did not use the same language as Paul did in clarifying the directive, but he did nonetheless give us further light on the subject. For that light we must go to Luke chapter 10, which contains the fuller treatment of the same incident. The lawyer who was tempting the Lord asked a further question: "And who is my neighbour?" (v. 29). The Savior answered with a parable that defines the love of a neighbor and allowed the lawyer to identify the definition for which he had asked. We call that parable "The Good Samaritan," a parable much more about what love is than who neighbors are.

A certain man had fallen among thieves and was stripped of raiment, wounded, and left for dead. He was passed by men of noble position, but a despised Samaritan stopped, bound up his wounds, put him on his own beast, took him to an inn, and paid his bills (see Luke 10:25–37).

The Samaritan loved this wounded neighbor "as himself," and so he treated him as he would want to be treated. He gave the man a bed equal to his own and treatment in general of as good a quality as he himself would want. He inconvenienced himself for the comfort of another. He *identified* with him and therefore gave all that was necessary for his comfort, as if the comfort were to be his own. The Savior finished the parable with the admonition to the lawyer: "Go, and do thou likewise" (v. 37).

There is little doubt in my mind that the words "Love thy neighbour as thyself" are simply a restatement of the Golden Rule. The words "as thyself" are an admonition to identify with others and seek their comfort as you would your own. When we read this commandment as "Love thy neighbour *and* thyself," we encourage a self-awareness that may stop us from truly seeing the needs of others and therefore may prevent us from exercising the discipline to put their needs above our own. If I might paraphrase Paul, I would render this scripture in modern language as "Love your neighbor the way you love yourself, wanting no ill for him as you want none for yourself, feeling with him his sorrows and joys as you do for yourself, concerned for his survival and welfare as much as you are for yourself."

It is a facet of the natural man that we are self-concerned. The Lord knows our tendency to put ourselves first, and he is telling us to feel as intensely about others.

Most of us may "tsk-tsk" when we watch a natural disaster on the evening news, but we are much more greatly dismayed to find out that we're out of milk and have to make a special visit to a convenience store before morning.

It is this unfortunate truth about our acquired human nature that the Lord uses as a frame of reference when he tells us *how* to love our neighbor. He uses the same frame of reference at other times when he wants us to know that what he is telling us to do is only a matter of benefiting ourselves.

Reading the scripture in Matthew as three commandments leads us away from what seems the primary purpose of the verses—to teach us, as so many scriptures do, to abase ourselves in order to be exalted and to emphasize that strength is made perfect in weakness, that love seeks not its own and "vaunteth not itself."

King Benjamin spoke the truth when he said that the knowledge of God and his goodness should awaken us to a sense of our nothingness, as it did Moses and Enoch and Jeremiah and Abraham. The Lord's response, in his great love for us, is to ignore our current fallen state, just as he did those prophets of old. He will, as he did through King Benjamin, offer us salvation through the atonement of Christ, through our trusting in the Lord and being diligent in keeping his commandments.

It is significant to me that this second commandment—to love our neighbor—was preceded by the words "And the second is like unto it." The first commandment was to love God. The second is like unto it. It is like unto it because it is virtually the same commandment. Elsewhere in the book of Matthew we are taught, "Inasmuch as ye have done it unto one of the least of these my brethren, ye have done it unto me" (Matt. 25:40).

His love is the greatest of all sources of energy. If we will also energize by loving, he will accept it as sharing his goal to bring about the eternal life of man, and he will consider it "like unto it."

There was true understanding of this principle in a favorite old poem:

Abou Ben Adhem (may his tribe increase!)
Awoke one night from a deep dream of peace,
And saw, within the moonlight in his room,
Making it rich, and like a lily in bloom,
An Angel writing in a book of gold:
Exceeding peace had made Ben Adhem bold,
And to the Presence in the room he said,
"What writest thou?" The Vision raised its head,
And with a look made of all sweet accord
Answered, "The names of those who love the Lord."
"And is mine one?" said Abou. "Nay, not so,"
Replied the Angel. Abou spoke more low,
But cheerily still; and said, "I pray thee, then,
Write me as one that loves his fellow men."
The Angel wrote, and vanished. The next night,
It came again with a great wakening light,
And showed the names whom love of God had blessed,
And, lo! Ben Adhem's name led all the rest![1]

Let us not mingle God's precious "great" commandments with worldly philosophies that lead to a greater consciousness of self. This great statement of the Savior's was, I'm sure, never intended to be a denial of the Christian paradox.

The Lord did not command us to love ourselves. He simply acknowledged that we do. All of us do. It is a human fact that we seek our own comfort, seek our own survival. Or, as the prophet David O. McKay said it, "Nature's law demands us to do everything with self in view. Self-preservation is the first law of mortal life. But Jesus says: 'He that findeth his life

1. James Henry Leigh Hunt, "Abou Ben Adhem," as quoted in Jack M. Lyon et al., comps., *Best-Loved Poems of the LDS People* (Salt Lake City: Deseret Book Co., 1996), 104.

shall lose it: and he that loseth his life for my sake shall find it.' (Matt. 10:39.)"[2]

And as Spencer W. Kimball said with plainness, "We did not come on earth to love ourselves."[3]

The reading of Matthew 22:39 to include a third great commandment is done by those who are motivated to free us from self-condemnation. But self-love is not the antidote for self-condemnation. It is simply the opposite manifestation of the same spiritual disease: self-consciousness.

Self-hatred, as a matter of fact, is the most intense form of self-love, because it is total self-absorption, total preoccupation with seeking our own comfort.

Condemnation, self-imposed or otherwise, can only be overcome by the atonement of the Lord Jesus Christ, from which we benefit fully only when we show humble obedience.

The Lord knows our natural man. He knows how much we worry about our own needs. He knows that we are self-concerned, self-aware—in other words, self-loving. Only the guidance of the Spirit will help us overcome that mindset and move us toward availing ourselves of the atonement of Christ. The only way to achieve that relationship with the Spirit is to keep the commandments, all of which can be summarized by loving the Lord with everything we've got, and loving other people in the same way that we love ourselves—seeking their comfort and their spiritual survival. Our relationship with the Spirit is like our relationship with others—a matter of long-handled spoons. The Lord used the fact of our "natural" self-love to teach us how to care for others. It is still as true as it

---

2. *Gospel Ideals: Selections from the Discourses of David O. McKay* (Salt Lake City: The Improvement Era, 1953), 297.

3. *The Teachings of Spencer W. Kimball*, ed. Edward L. Kimball (Salt Lake City: Bookcraft, 1982), 243.

ever was that we must lose ourselves to find ourselves. There is no "I" in peace.

"This know also, that in the last days perilous times shall come. For men shall be lovers of their own selves" (2 Tim. 3:1–2).

THE NINTH KEY

"Always Remember Him"

Though other faiths may call God "Father," Latter-day Saints are unique, I believe, in the understanding of that principle and what it means to us. Our spirits are the literal spiritual offspring of our Father whose dwelling place is in heaven.

The statement "I am a child of God" is an acknowledgment of our most treasured blessing: our potential to become like him. It is not a statement that we *are* already gods, only that that wonderful, beautiful, hopeful potential exists. It is not a statement that we must become like him on our own merits alone, but only that the wonder, the beauty, and the hope of the Atonement is available to us.

Because of that atonement, every child of God will be resurrected someday. Our spirits will be, as David described "redeemed . . . out of all distress" (1 Kgs. 1:29). It is an unconditional blessing of great magnitude. Our resurrected bodies will be wonderful, new, incorruptible, everlasting temples for our spirits. Those spirits were begotten by our Father in Heaven. God the Father cares for those spirits in a way that only a parent could: single-mindedly, unconditionally; "For behold, this is my work and my glory—to bring to pass the immortality and eternal life of man" (Moses 1:39).

God's plan was not to give us "status" in this life but to give us *opportunity* to prepare to be with him again (see Alma 34:32). He wanted us to be able to make that preparation by choices within whatever limited or expanded environment in which we find ourselves here on earth. He wanted us all to share in the inheritance of his name and estate. He has a mighty inheritance to offer! His estate includes all knowledge, all power, and, most important, the ability to generate that which he has generated: spirit bodies.

The inheritance, however, belongs only to the birthright son: Jesus the Christ.[1] The Father has endowed the rest of us with many wonderful blessings, but the inheritance of the kingdom belongs to Jehovah. Jehovah is the eldest son, and so full of devotion to his Father and charity for us that he desired the will of the Father—to have *all* of God's children share equally in the birthright with him (see D&C 34:3). Nevertheless, since he was the heir, he had to make us all his own children—an adoption process as it were, so that *he* could bestow the inheritance on us and we could be joint heirs with him (see Gal. 4:4–7).

The "catch" was that sinlessness was required to have the full inheritance of God the Father, "for no unclean thing can

---

1. Hugh B. Brown said, "Chief among that vast assembly was Jehovah, the same who would become the Christ Child, the Redeemer. He was the Firstborn among the spirits, and by birthright was both heir and leader" (Conference Report, October 1963, 92). And Elder Bruce R. McConkie taught in *Mormon Doctrine*, "Christ is the heir of God" (Salt Lake City: Bookcraft, 1966). The scriptures bear ample witness of this fact, as in Hebrews 1:2, 4: God "hath in these last days spoken unto us by his Son, whom he hath appointed heir of all things, by whom also he made the worlds; . . . Being made so much better than the angels, as he hath by inheritance obtained a more excellent name than they."

dwell there, or dwell in his presence" (Moses 6:57; see also Alma 11:37). And all of us knew that, being free to choose, we all—except Christ—would occasionally make mistakes. None of the rest of us would make it through this life without sinning. The law of justice was such that by paying a price, sins could be atoned for and we could be one with Christ and with God the Father. But the atoning price could only be paid by the Messiah's sinless suffering and sacrifice (see Alma 5:21; 2 Ne. 2:8). The only route to the miraculous adoption by our elder brother was for that marvelously generous, sinless, birthright brother to pay the price—not only for Adam's transgression but for *our* sins—so that we could approach the Father without our sins.

"Father, thy will be done," Jesus said, choosing to pay that price (Moses 4:2).

"For ye are bought with a price: therefore glorify God" (1 Cor. 6:20).

This great gift—this fact of being a child of God and this potential to become a child of Christ and therefore joint heir with Christ to the kingdom of our Father—should be a cause for incalculable gratitude. In the words of King Benjamin, "O how [we] ought to thank [our] Heavenly King!" (Mosiah 2:19).

This great, divine gift is reason all by itself for each of us to wear a badge that says "I am loved and grateful."

This is the good news—the fulness of the gospel that the scriptures contain: that we can be his by doing his will.

"Not every one that saith unto me, Lord, Lord, shall enter into the kingdom of heaven; but he that doeth the will of my Father who is in heaven" (3 Ne. 14:21).

If ever we are searching for a definition of perfect love, we have only to contemplate that gift of the Atonement. Christ endured nails, sweating blood, derision, and death itself—

descending in agony, as he told Joseph Smith, below them all—and this because *we* deserved what he endured, in spite of the fact that he deserved not a whit of it himself (see D&C 122:8). He had only one thing to gain from it: His suffering made it possible to share with us what was rightfully his—the inheritance of God the Father. No wonder we "stand all amazed."[2]

But we have a problem.

Our problem is that we *forget* that the inheritance was the Savior's by birthright. We tend to take pride in being children of God, and that causes us to believe that God the Father's wealth is *ours* by birthright. While we should be in awe of being the spirit children of God the Father and should take every opportunity to remind one another of the wonderful love and potential that parentage provides, still it is imperative that we understand that we are not the *birthright* children.

If we believe that somehow our filial connection to God the Father gives us a *right* to his inheritance, instead of just the potential for it, we will seriously undervalue the gift and the love of Christ.

We focus on our royal birth because we feel unique in our Latter-day Saint understanding of it. But for the good of our souls and our eternal life, it is imperative that we focus on our royal *re*birth. Becoming the sons and daughters of Christ must have our humble effort. We do this by taking upon us his name and his love and vowing never to betray either.

We become the beneficiaries of "the adoption of children by Jesus Christ to himself, according to the good pleasure of his will" (Eph. 1:5).

---

2. *Hymns of The Church of Jesus Christ of Latter-day Saints* (Salt Lake City: The Church of Jesus Christ of Latter-day Saints, 1985), no. 193.

In truth, the restored gospel is unique in understanding *re*birth as well.

This most basic and most profound doctrine is a necessary and clarifying reminder of what we mean when we say, "I am a child of God." To receive the inheritance, we must take the name of Christ upon us, by ordinance and by action. It requires the humble commitment of our hearts.

Because the philosophies of men are sometimes easily mingled with scripture, and because the world tells us that we must think well of ourselves, we sometimes look to our status as children of God to get the self-esteem the world tells us we need. It appears to us that perhaps we can ride both horses: we get what the world says to get, but we get it from the gospel. It sounds like the best of both worlds. In essence, it becomes "okay" to have pride so long as we have pride in being created by God and in his image. We tell ourselves that pride is a matter of thinking we are better than others, and that if we take self-importance in something that includes all mankind, then it's not really pride. It's acceptable. Right?

Oh, how careful we must be with that kind of thinking. Even if it includes the entire human race, anything that stops us from seeing the absolute greatness of God in contrast to ourselves will prove to be a barrier to the self-abasement we must achieve before him.

If the world tells us to think well of ourselves, we must not buy into it and mingle the doctrine of ultimate potential with that philosophy of men. Indeed, if we serve God with all our heart, might, mind, and strength, we may, *by his grace,* one day become perfect in Christ (see Moro. 10:32). But it is not a matter of *self*-worth. Rather it is a matter of our great worth to our Father in Heaven and to our Savior, Jesus Christ, and to those who love us in mortality.

We must not talk in terms of our own status. We must

resist the temptation to mingle the worldly philosophies with the doctrines of the Kingdom. It will not bring us the peace for which we yearn. It will leave us either with an insatiable desire to be wonderful or it will leave us exhausted from *measuring* what we do. We need to think instead, I am a child of God. I am loved and grateful—even in my fallen state.

Status is unnecessary. The peace of the atonement of Christ can take the place of both measurement and paralyzing guilt in our lives. Striving to become fully complete children of Christ as well as children of our Father in Heaven is an easy yoke and a light burden. We have eternity; there are no clocks in the garden of eternal life. And we are so very greatly loved. Alma expressed it so beautifully: "Yea, I know that I am nothing; as to my strength I am weak; therefore I will not boast of myself, but I will boast of my God, for in his strength I can do all things" (Alma 26:12).

THE TENTH KEY

Remember That God Isn't the Source of Your Stress

In this section we have dealt with the scriptural concepts that are mingled with the philosophies of men and that consequently result in self-focus. Chapters 8 and 9 caution us about two scriptural concepts that are used to *legitimize* these man-made philosophies. This tenth key to our happiness is to gain a correct understanding as we read and understand some of the scriptures that are *blamed as creating a need* for these philosophies. They are the scriptures that are believed to rob human beings of their contentment, seen to set them up for stress and frustration, and viewed as evidence of a relentless God from whose unattainable demands man must be given relief. They are the scriptures that command, "Be ye therefore perfect" (Matt. 5:48; see also Gen. 17:1).

Just as we saw that the scriptural phrase about loving ourselves is a frame of reference to tell us how to love others, and just as we examined the doctrine to learn that being a child of God is a source of love, hope, and belonging but does not encourage status and pride, so we must take the scriptures as a whole to understand the meaning of the words "Be ye therefore perfect." I believe that it is clear from both ancient scripture and modern prophets that these words are a great and precious promise—not an invitation into the frustrating world of the impossible.

Recently my husband was talking to a group of new missionaries at the Missionary Training Center and the topic was obedience. His text was 1 Samuel 15, in which Saul was commanded to destroy the entire Amalekite nation—everyone and everything. When he conquered them, however, Saul decided to destroy not quite everything but to spare the king and the best of the animals. Saul reported to the prophet, "I have obeyed the commandment of the Lord." My husband paused then and asked this question of the group: "What do you think? Had Saul obeyed the commandment of the Lord?" A missionary near the front said defensively in behalf of Saul, "About 90 percent!"

My heart filled with love for the young missionary, who was generously trying to give partial credit for Saul's failing to obey the Lord. But the simple fact is that Saul was disobedient. He *chose* to make changes in what the Lord commanded.

What if, instead, while Saul was giving the best he had to offer and trying with all his might, Agag the king had escaped and some of the animals had run away? What then? The result would have been the same as what actually happened. Right? Agag and the animals alive? Oh, no! It might have been the same for Agag and the animals, but not in the most important respect for Saul. Saul would have been obedient because his *heart* was right. And likely his house would have remained faithful, and perhaps they would have remained kings in Israel for the rest of their days. The Lord does not ask whether we fought the best battle—whether our abilities are keen or our result was perfection. He asks if our heart was in the fight.

Two verses in 2 Chronicles are revelatory in this regard.

2 Chronicles 15:17 records the leadership battle of Asa, a later king in Judah, who tried mightily to cleanse his people of pagan worship: "But the high places were not taken away out of Israel: nevertheless the heart of Asa was perfect all his days."

Amaziah, a later king in Judah, was just the opposite: "And he did that which was right in the sight of the Lord, but not with a perfect heart" (2 Chr. 25:2).

Or as Joseph Smith has said: "Therefore the man who has within himself [spiritual life] is nearer [perfection] than the man who has morality alone. The latter can never reach perfection, the former must."[1]

In *Mormon Doctrine,* Bruce R. McConkie suggests that there are really two meanings to the word *perfect* in the scriptures: one finite and achievable in this life with the help of the Spirit, and one infinite and achievable only as a celestial being.[2]

It is my belief that the mortally achievable one has to do not with checklists but with the heart.[3] For, as it is also recorded in 2 Chronicles, "The eyes of the Lord run to and fro throughout the whole earth, to shew himself strong in the behalf of them whose heart is perfect toward him" (16:9).

The Sermon on the Mount, in which the Savior includes the "troublesome" command of perfection, is indeed about the heart. I feel certain that when the Lord talks about righteousness, it is the heart which he means. In Matthew 5:20 he says, "Except your righteousness shall exceed the righteous-

---

1. *Teachings of the Prophet Joseph Smith,* ed. Joseph Fielding Smith (Salt Lake City: The Church of Jesus Christ of Latter-day Saints, 1938), 346, n. 3.

2. See Bruce R. McConkie, *Mormon Doctrine,* 2d ed. (Salt Lake City: Bookcraft, 1966), 567.

3. I should qualify that statement by saying I believe that checklists have their place—in "to do" lists, in mortal goal setting, and in progress evaluation.

ness of the scribes and Pharisees, ye shall in no case enter into the kingdom of heaven."

The scribes and Pharisees were the champion checklisters. By a heavenly bookkeeping system, perhaps *no one* could be more "righteous" than they. Nevertheless, the Lord sees righteousness not in result but in root. Ironically, the truly righteous must see themselves as not perfect at all: Blessed are the meek, the mourner, the poor in spirit, and they who do hunger and thirst after righteousness. And the Lord sees this as *exceeding* the checklisters' righteousness.

As a mid-sermon summary, the Lord plainly tells his listeners what he told them in the beginning: how he will reward the poor, meek, hungry, thirsty mourners. It is just another way to say that they will inherit the earth, receive the kingdom of heaven, be mercifully filled with comfort, and see God. He tells them that they will be *therefore* perfect. In other words, this love, this selflessness that he has been talking about—this perfect heart—is required if man is to receive the reward of becoming ultimately as his Father which is in heaven. These attributes of humility are the motivators to unlimited, unmeasured diligence within our competence. It is humility that leads us to take on the easy yoke and the light burden. These are the ways to release all the resistance to his direction and to receive his love. These are the paths to the promised gift of perfection. Not our own puny power, with our deeds diligently listed on a checklist, but his generous, charitable omnipotence given to those who truly love him: his children of perfect heart.

As I have taught institute classes, students have sometimes asked me, "How do you get to this point of hungering and thirsting after righteousness? What if you just don't have the desire? What if it just doesn't appeal to you? I've heard that the Lord can give you the desire, as well, if you just pray for it."

I answer that it seems to me that if we are praying for it, there is at least the nubbin of desire within us already. Alma says that even a desire to believe can grow. But that small desire, that prayer for belief, *that* is *our* department. The Lord can't give us everything; if he were to do so, where is the doctrine of agency? If righteousness does not appeal to us, he will surely not force us into it, even if we ask him to. The condition of our heart is that for which we are most accountable.

As Elder Neal A. Maxwell of the Quorum of the Twelve said in his October 1996 conference address, your desire is all your own and the very core of your accountability: "Of course our genes, circumstances, and environments matter very much, and they shape us significantly. Yet there remains an inner zone in which we are sovereign, unless we abdicate. In this zone lies the essence of our individuality and our personal accountability. . . . Like it or not, therefore, reality requires that we acknowledge our responsibility for our desires."[4] If you desire righteousness, you must plant that desire as a seed. The planting of the desire is done through commitment. Through the process of covenant the Lord gives us opportunities to commit, and that to which we are truly and *faithfully* willing to commit—that is where our heart is. Sometimes we don't know our own heart (as in the case of my institute and MTC students who think they have no desire for righteousness but find themselves on their knees praying for it) and in order for peace to come, we must not be kidding ourselves about our hearts (see chapter 3). We find out something about ourselves when we make commitments. As we make commitments, we find out where our hearts are. Alma talked about the growth of the seed of desire and compared it to a seed bursting within

---

4. *Ensign,* November 1996, 21.

us and bringing forth good fruit. That growth, which comes from our "experiment upon the word" tells us that our hearts are reaching toward perfection (see Alma 32:27).

Of course, if we reject the opportunity to commit, or if we make commitments we don't keep—well, that tells us something about our hearts as well. Something a little less pleasant to know. Remember the rich young man in the New Testament and how he went away sorrowing. Perhaps it was what he had learned about the condition of his heart that brought him sorrow. The opportunity to commit is the opportunity to know our own hearts. In any event, all hearts are not equal, because they are our *own* creation and receive from God only what they have invited in. It is the *heart* that determines whether our performance will reach toward perfection in this life. I use the words "reach toward" advisedly. The Lord reminds us that faith the size of a mustard seed can move mountains. The reason this is true is because it is not the power of our faith that moves mountains of the spirit, but the fact of our faith in the power of *God.* Even a mustard-seed's-worth of desire can lead us to faith in the power and perfection of God. I think that's what Alma meant when he said that you could plant the seed if you have "no more than desire to believe" (Alma 32:27). If we believe that it must be our own power, our own "perfect" faith, that could move the mountain, we may live this whole life in its shadow. If, however, we understand that it is God's perfection of power that is "mightier than all the earth," and bring ourselves with lowliness of heart to understand that, then that mountain may be removed and we can live forever in bright, unshaded light (see 1 Ne. 4:1).

One of my favorite verses about Solomon is in 1 Kings 10, in which it says that all the earth sought Solomon to hear his wisdom which God had put in *his heart.* We who think in terms of human wonder and intellect think of wisdom as a thing of the mind. But it was Solomon's *heart* into which the Lord was able to put wisdom. And it must be our hearts into which the Lord puts our earthly level of perfection. Not our minds, not our muscles, not our training or our beauty or anything that is seen of men. It must be put into a perfect heart. Or at least, as Alma reminds us, a heart that has a *desire* to be perfect.

I am continually humbled, as we work at the Missionary Training Center in Provo, by some of the sister missionaries. The wardrobe requirements are somewhat less defined for sisters than they are for elders. More latitude is given and more judgment is required. The Brethren, however, have been nonetheless emphatic in their charge to the sister missionaries regarding their appearance when they go forth to represent the Lord. It has been made clear that they should be dressy, neat, conservative, and classic. It is common in an environment of so much latitude to discount the charge of the Brethren in favor of individual taste and ease. It is less common, but more thrilling, to see those sisters whose hearts are desiring to be perfect. They try with all their might to comply with the directives of the Brethren. It is a kind of miracle to watch how the Lord blesses the sisters' efforts when self-awareness is not the issue.

Occasionally we hear in the Church that there is much depression and much stress because of the commandment to be perfect. Some see the Lord as a relentless observer instead of the comforter of those whose hearts are perfect. They mingle great principles of promise with the worldly practice of self-awareness.

In the interest of the peace for which we yearn, we would all do well to recognize that the commandment to be perfect is not the problem. The problem is not that the Lord is relentless, not that the Church is relentless, not even that friends and neighbors are relentless. It is that our search for self-esteem is relentless. And the search for self-esteem is conducted by our "natural man." *We* may want to relieve our stress by lowering the standard. But God knows the needs of our hearts and tells us instead to raise our level of patience.

Elder Neal A. Maxwell, who has helped in so many ways our understanding of this principle, has said: "In a kingdom where perfection is an eventual expectation, our feelings of anxiety and inadequacy should not surprise us. . . . There is really no way present prophets can describe where we must yet go without creating a sense of distance. We are not merely journeying next door or even across town."[5]

The route to peace is not through believing ourselves perfect, after all. Quite the contrary. The route to peace is through humility to repentance to finding mercy. It is a function of the heart.

An institute student once pointed out to me that the Lord told the people of the Book of Mormon so often that he required their hearts that surely that is the reason a later confused Lamanite population cut out the hearts of humans to offer as a sacrifice. I think my student may well have something there.

The commandment to have a perfect heart is the Lord's way of showing us the route to the peace for which we yearn.

The chronicler of ancient Judah understood this principle when he told the story of Asa, the righteous king, and the people of his country who joined with him to try to bring repentance to the nation of Judah: "For they had sworn with all their heart and sought him with their whole desire; and he

---

5. Neal A. Maxwell, *Notwithstanding My Weakness* (Salt Lake City: Deseret Book Co., 1981), 1.

was found of them: and the Lord gave them rest round about" (2 Chron. 15:15).

The apostle Paul understood this principle when he recorded: "And he said unto me, My grace is sufficient for thee: for my strength is made perfect in weakness. Most gladly therefore will I rather glory in my infirmities, that the power of Christ may rest upon me" (2 Cor. 12:9).

The Savior wanted us *all* to understand this principle when he commanded that we pray, "For thine is the kingdom, and the power, and the glory, for ever. Amen" (Matt. 6:9).

PART 4

The Keys of Choice

"It must needs be that there was an opposition; . . . Wherefore, man could not act for himself save it should be that he was enticed by the one or the other."

—2 Nephi 2:15–16

THE ELEVENTH KEY

Short-Term Comfort Isn't Joy

We earlier discussed making a commitment to seek gratitude, the foundation of peace (see chapter 7). We talked about the beautiful irony: that in being grateful for our gifts and for our being loved, we see our own merit as well as our own worth to others. That kind of gratitude is what lets us say and feel, "I'm glad I'm me." That's not a comparative statement, just a grateful statement. The scriptures counsel, "To every man is given a gift by the Spirit of God. . . . And ye must give thanks unto God in the Spirit for whatsoever blessing ye are blessed with" (D&C 46:11, 32). That kind of gratitude is a self-acknowledgment but not an absorbed self-awareness.

When we are glad to be ourselves, there is no threat in enlarging ourselves. Growth in what we are grateful for may be challenging, but it is also thrilling. Our attitude becomes like that of King Benjamin's people, who "all cried with one voice, saying: Yea, we believe all the words which thou hast spoken unto us; and also, we know of their surety and truth, because of the Spirit of the Lord Omnipotent, which has wrought a mighty change in us" (Mosiah 5:2).

It is a short and easy distance, however, for the adversary to take that grateful focus of "I'm glad I'm me and I'm excited to be more" to a guarded and hoarding determination: "I've got to protect what I am right now, because if I change it will mean that what I am now is not good enough." When the Spirit would encourage us toward the "mighty change," Satan presents the attractive opposite: "I've gotta be me!"

Missionaries in the field are greatly handicapped if they have the "I've gotta be me" focus. A mission is a time when great discipline is required. Daily schedules may not be what the missionary is accustomed to. Shyness may make tracting difficult. Fear of rejection is real. Sacrifice of worldly pleasures is painful. The experience requires changes in behavior. When the missionaries make the necessary changes, it is liberating. They find that within the order required they can accomplish much more than they believed possible. In doing so much, they build up their competence and then can extend their diligence into a whole new range of competence—spiraling upward until they become the man or woman their home ward sees upon their return. It is revealing, but not uncommon, for such a young man or woman to say, "I'm so *grateful* that I was able to serve this mission."

All of this is in contrast to the young man or woman who believes that shielding self-esteem must be foremost. It hurts to get up at 6:00 or 6:30. It can hurt even more to go to bed at 10:30. Often a missionary will guardedly focus on who he *is* and determine that he is "a night person" or "not a people person," or "just not a student," or "not as spiritual as others." This or that, a missionary will sometimes say, is simply "not my nature." Over and over, a mission president hears variations of the theme "I've gotta be me!"

It would be valuable if instead the missionary would carefully read Mosiah 3:19, that beautiful scriptural verse that describes the natural man and his opposite, "a saint through the atonement of Christ . . . , [who] becometh as a child, submissive, meek, humble, patient, full of love, willing to submit to all things which the Lord seeth fit to inflict upon him, even as a child doth submit to his father."

This is wise direction for all of us, of course, not just for full-time missionaries. If we follow this counsel, we allow the Holy Ghost to lead us to a mighty change by way of the atonement of Christ. Perhaps it would be more accurate to say *through* a mighty change, for it comes incrementally, line upon line, as our hearts develop a huge desire to be like him.

Each of us must ask ourselves the question Alma asked those he taught: "And now behold, I ask of you, my brethren of the church, have ye spiritually been born of God? Have ye received his image in your countenances? Have ye experienced this mighty change in your hearts?" (Alma 5:14).

The attitude we need to cultivate is not "You've got to feel good about yourself" or "You've got to know yourself and be true to yourself" or "You're special just the way you are" or any other way of saying "I've gotta be me." The attitude that builds strength can be more aptly expressed in such terms as "You've got to feel good about *God*" and "You've got to know *God* and be true to *him*" and "You are special to him and so you need not fear risking growth."

A missionary often serves as living proof that focus on "I'm terrific just the way I am" is at least as damning as focus on "I'm awful." The two are, in fact, different manifestations of the same thing. They are both a self-consciousness that prevents a focus outside oneself—prevents a focus on gratitude and growth.

Love from others reassures us that it is not necessary to be terrific. We feel grateful to be someone who is loved and want to grow ever more toward a full experience of knowing God and knowing the love of God. We experience the mighty change in our hearts. The Spirit aids us in our effort and puts no timetable or checklist on our progress. And then "the God of all grace, who hath called us unto his eternal glory by Christ Jesus, after that ye have suffered a while, [will] make you perfect, stablish, strengthen, settle you" (1 Pet. 5:10).

When we were on our mission in Montreal, the sister missionaries brought to church a young woman to whom they had asked the "Golden Questions" on the Metro. The young woman was a picture of despair. Her earthly parents had not wanted her, and she was completely alone in the world. She had been addicted to illegal drugs. She was poorly dressed, and her hair was unkempt. If ever there was someone who needed to know of her Heavenly Father's love, it was this young woman. And the sister missionaries delivered that knowledge to her. The young woman was incredibly grateful, and at first she was as dependent as she was appreciative. She clung to the sisters who had taught her. When she was with them she wouldn't let them out of her sight, and she was totally reliant upon them. She was dull and lifeless in her affect and hung on their arms until they would come to us and ask what they should do. Little by little, the Saints in the ward gave their love and support to the sister. They got her a job and literally taught her what to do on the job. They taught her some basic hygiene, and we thought we saw some improvement. But it was slow and laborious work for her to change. When we left Quebec, this young woman told us that someday she wanted to go on a mission like the sisters who had taught her. She wanted others to know about being a child of God. At the time we thought it was an ambitious dream, but we smiled and I hugged her when we left.

Now fast-forward three years. There's a mission reunion at our home. We're all hanging around the table by the food, and at the other end of the table there is a striking girl. She's dressed in white pants and a starched open-collar shirt. Her hair is lovely and her makeup perfect. She's accompanied by a young man who is obviously crazy about her. I hear someone talking about their getting married as she says she's not sure if she's ready. She seems very independent. I look at her. I look at my husband. The girl looks familiar somehow, but I can tell my husband is having the same trouble I am. She couldn't be one of our sister missionaries. Surely we'd remember. We're tortured by it, and she sees that we are. She relieves us.

"President and Sister Rasband, can I have a hug? I'm—I'm Suzette" (I've changed her name to protect her privacy). Well, had we guessed all day we would not have guessed that!

We said, "You can't mean it!" She said, "Yes. I do. Remember I told you I wanted to go on a mission? Well, I went. It was wonderful! Life is very different for me now than it was when I saw you last. The Lord has blessed me so much since that day the sisters found me on the Metro."

Suzette had very little to give to the Lord when she decided to submit to the mighty change. She had so little "self" that one would think she would guard it mightily. But she was so grateful for the love of the sister missionaries that she was willing to risk *everything*—little as it was. Her gratitude created in her a perfect heart. Not perfect in the sense that it had been unblemished, but perfect in that it was totally devoted to the Lord. By any checklist she had thus far failed miserably in life. But not in the true test of the heart, once she had accepted the gospel. Following the Lord was worth everything to her, so she opened herself to the Holy Spirit and left off the "natural man" and became "a saint through the atonement of Christ the Lord" (Mosiah 3:19). Not for one moment did Suzette resist the mighty change that the Lord had in mind for her. Never once did she treasure her control or feel threatened by the Lord's commands. Her heart was so into it that in three years from the time we left Quebec, she had served a mission and turned from a crawling caterpillar into a flying butterfly. I'm sure she made mistakes along the way, but "relying wholly upon the merits of him who is mighty to save," she submitted to the change and it was indeed mighty (2 Ne. 31:19).

When we say—or feel—"I've gotta be me," we can't become the butterfly because our caterpillar does not welcome the cocoon. We must instead be so grateful that we love the Lord so much that his countenance shows in ours. It is the very opposite of guarding our "self." It is peace.

"For they had sworn with all their heart, and sought him with their whole desire; and he was found of them: and the Lord gave them rest round about" (2 Chron. 15:15).

"Have ye received his image in your countenances? Have ye experienced this mighty change in your hearts?" (Alma 5:14).

THE TWELFTH KEY

Peace Is a Gift of the Spirit

There is such well-meaning intent in those who would give us peace made simple. Unfortunately, peace made simple is synonymous with peace made impossible. Perhaps the most virulent example of attractive opposites to the Lord's way is the urging that we can "have it all"—that choice is unnecessary. That worldly philosophy is, of course, the exact opposite of "Sacrifice brings forth the blessings of heaven."[1] President Spencer W. Kimball said it this way: "I tell you, when we get away from the sacrifice, we have slipped a cog. . . . Sacrifices for a just cause make character."[2]

Sadly, character is often less important to us than avoiding a feeling of deprivation. But peace comes only with character—not with indulgence.

In today's society we tend to identify "having it all" as a women's issue. It is not, however, a feminine phenomenon.

---

1. *Hymns of The Church of Jesus Christ of Latter-day Saints* (Salt Lake City: The Church of Jesus Christ of Latter-day Saints, 1985), no. 27.

2. *The Teachings of Spencer W. Kimball* (Salt Lake City: Bookcraft, 1982), 179.

Men, too, give way to it every day. For both, it is accompanied by such light-hearted sayings as "Life's too short" or "You only go 'round once." More often and more seriously, we hear, "Why should I be deprived?" It manifests itself in all kinds of ugly questions:

"Just because I have taken on the responsibility of children, why should I be deprived of my dream?"

"Just because I'm devoting myself to my career, why should I be deprived of motherhood?"

"Just because my wife is disabled, why should I be deprived of a full and active life?"

"Just because I chose a career that doesn't pay well, why should I be deprived of luxury?"

"Just because we've been living together for years, why should I be deprived of a big wedding?"

The list is endless. If you attune your ear to it, you will hear this formula sentence several times in every day: it begins "just because (fill in the blank)" and ends "why should I be deprived of (fill in the blank)?"

It seems to be the human condition to feel deprived. No matter how hard we try to fight that condition by telling ourselves that we can have it all, the truth remains: we can only fight those negative feelings with an appreciation for the blessings inherent in sacrifice. (You will notice, of course, that the opposite of a feeling of deprivation is a feeling of gratitude, which feeling we have already identified as the fundamental key to peace.)

All my life I have heard the old Puritan adage that a man will never grow rich until he is willing to be poor without feeling deprived. I always understood it on the financial level, although whether I was always successful at living it is quite another question. There came a day, however, when it dawned on me that this is not just a financial law.

The spiritual implications with regard to sacrifice are enormous. As I realized that, I began to try to put the law to work in the areas where I was demanding more of life—the ways in which I felt deprived. Slowly, I came to understand that:

- I needed to be more grateful.
- I needed an eternal perspective.
- I needed a better understanding of the principle of agency.

First, let's discuss the principle of gratitude. Happiness requires gratitude, and gratitude creates happiness. It is axiomatic. A feeling of deprivation is a focus on what we *don't* have. The problem of ingratitude can be devastating materially, leading as it does to debt and greed, but on a spiritual level ingratitude is even worse. It is true damnation. We may have have sung "Count Your Many Blessings" so many times that it seems trite and Pollyanna-like, but it preaches a true doctrine. It is in our best interest to cultivate gratitude in our lives. It is unwise to be ungrateful.

Second, the matter of eternal perspective: life is not too short, it is too long. It is forever. You don't go 'round once; it is one eternal round. Remember the garden we talked about in chapter five—the garden we want so desperately to get into? Remember there are no clocks in the garden and that all the goodness of eternal life awaits us there. We have forever to get the goodies, so to speak, and the only thing that will keep us from them is giving up on the effort. Unfortunately, when we see life as too short to be deprived, we are tempted to give up. If I might use the formula sentence to make a point, we begin to ask foolishly, "Just because I can have an eternity of joy, why should I be deprived of worldly rewards now?" This mindset is obviously destructive; those who live life with that attitude are indeed shortsighted. As the Lord said, "Verily I say unto you, They have their reward" (Matt. 6:2).

Third, it is our understanding of our own agency that liberates us most surely to give up our feelings of deprivation. When we comprehend how very free we are to choose and use our eternal perspective to make choices, we will begin to be grateful and therefore happy. We must "stand fast therefore in the liberty wherewith Christ hath made us free" (Gal. 5:1). God, in his infinite goodness, gave us the Atonement so that we could be free to choose, and we must choose wisely so that we do not forfeit that freedom (2 Ne. 2:26). To teach us this principle, God has made us free to choose everything in this life. Everything, that is, except two things: reality and mutually exclusive blessings.

Reality

The first thing that we are not free to choose is reality. We do not get to choose what is true and what isn't. Things are as they really are, whether or not we comprehend them or accept them. The reality is, for instance, that Joseph Smith saw God the Father and his Son Jesus Christ, two separate beings. They told him that he would restore eternal truths to the world. That is a reality. We can choose to accept it or reject it, but we cannot choose whether or not it happened. It happened. And the fact that it happened changes all the consequences of life in this dispensation.

The realities about ourselves at any given moment come under the same heading. We are what we are at the moment. No one can take it away from us, so we need not feel threatened; no one else can make more of it, so we need not feel pressured. Depending upon what we do with the current moment, the reality may change. But right now it is what it is. We cannot choose otherwise.

We are also *where* we are at the moment. Our circumstance may be changed in time, but in any given moment we cannot choose to be in a circumstance in which we are not. That is reality.

We are not free to choose the feelings of others. That, too, is reality. For that reason we may choose our behavior but may not choose the reaction of others to our behavior. I remember my children telling me that it was not fair that I gave them the free agency to make a bad choice and then was disappointed in their choice. They said at the time that that meant they were not *really* free, if I was still going to disapprove. "Oh, yes," I told them. "You were free to do whatever you chose, but you were not free to choose how *I* would feel about it. You knew at the outset that I didn't like the idea. Your choice didn't change that. When you make a choice, a whole package of consequences comes along. My feelings are just part of that package. It's reality, as far as you're concerned."

It is the same principle in operation as having a temple recommend. We are certainly free to choose to break the Word of Wisdom, or stay away from our meetings, or not pay tithing, but if we do, we can't have a temple recommend. The reality is that those things are required for a temple recommend. That reality is the environment of our choice.

All of life's realities are outside of our freedom to choose. I remember when one of my sons was a little boy and didn't want to go to school, he announced one Wednesday morning that it was Saturday and he didn't have to go to school. All the announcing in the world, however, did not change the fact that it was really Wednesday. We can laugh at the childlike ways of wanting to choose what truth is, but we so-called "grownups" try to do it in more subtle ways every day:

through denial, or hypocrisy, or false witness. When presented with a choice between two alternatives, we always want the third choice—the one that isn't ours to make, the choice to change reality. If it's Wednesday, we can choose to go to school or stay home from school, but we can't choose for it to be Saturday. It won't work. We are not free to choose reality.

Mutually Exclusive Blessings

Second, we are not free to choose mutually exclusive blessings. It is what some have called the "Garden of Eden" lesson.

If you are on your way to sacrament meeting and you see a man in the street who is injured and who will surely die if you do not attend him, you have a choice to make. Do you go to sacrament meeting—a commandment as well as a place where you will receive instruction and the fellowship of the Saints? Or do you miss the meeting in order to attend the dying man? It seems an obvious choice. The life of your "neighbor" is certainly more important. "Is it lawful to do good on the sabbath days . . . ?" (Mark 3:4). Of course.

There is great blessing attached to being the good Samaritan. You know you have done the will of the Lord, and the joy of that kind of service is great. But what of the blessing attached to attendance at sacrament meeting? Will you have that blessing? The answer is no. That blessing was sacrificed in order to get the greater one. You will never feel the Spirit that everyone says was wonderful during Brother Smith's talk, or know the great feeling of seeing the little Jones boy pass the sacrament for the very first time. You're familiar with those feelings, you've had them before, but you didn't get to be there to share them with the others that Sunday morning. You chose another blessing—a greater blessing to be sure—but a mutually exclusive blessing.

I am reminded of a conversation I had with a wonderfully diligent young elder one day in Montreal while his companion was being interviewed by my husband. He had been reading and rereading Doctrine and Covenants 18:16: "And now, if your joy will be great with one soul that you have brought unto me into the kingdom of my Father, how great will be your joy if you should bring many souls unto me!"

Like many of the cold countries of the world, Quebec was not very receptive to the missionaries and their message. It was not uncommon for our young men and women to tract for fifty or sixty hours a week and only rarely get in out of the sub-zero weather, let alone be invited for a return appointment. The slammed doors were not made easier by the letters the missionaries got from their friends who had been called to warm South American countries where they taught several discussions a day and baptized every week.

"It just doesn't seem fair, Sister Rasband. Why do they go to the place where they get all the joy and I work my head off to get spit on? I may baptize a few, but I'll never know as much joy as they do from their mission."

"Elder," I said, after thinking a moment, "you're right. You will never know the joy of baptizing hundreds of people on your mission. Your friends will know a joy that you won't. But there is more than one kind of joy. They will never know the joy you will know of standing with the Lord when it is tough to do. They will never know that they are capable of hanging in there no matter what. Some of them will never know what the blessing is that the Lord was talking about in the Sermon on the Mount: 'Blessed are ye, when men shall revile you, and persecute you, and shall say all manner of evil against you falsely, for my sake. Rejoice, and be exceeding glad: for great is your reward in heaven: for so persecuted they the prophets which were before you' (Matt. 5:11–12).

"Someday when you're a bishop or a stake president and the going gets tough, you will be well prepared for it because you know the kind of joy that you're getting here in Quebec. It may be different joy, but it's at least equally profound. The two blessings are mutually exclusive. By accepting your call to Quebec, you chose a whole set of blessings that ruled out some others. That's the way it works."

So far we have talked about easy choices—easy because they are momentous and obvious. There is no contest between seeing the Jones boy pass the sacrament for the first time and saving a fellowman's life. It is not so difficult to accept a call, knowing that's the set of blessings the Lord has in mind for you. You might, if you're unwise, mourn the lost blessings that were on the other side of the coin, but you will not have serious doubts as to the Lord's will.

What about the more difficult choices—difficult because they are less momentous or less obvious or both? I'll tell you about a little choice—a personal choice that I found myself having to make thirty-six different times. It involved mutually exclusive blessings, and it illustrates not only that you can't "have it all" but that the principle of agency is designed for our development in such a way as to make the choice sometimes less apparent as to just what sacrifice to make. Understanding the nature of this developmental design can help us give up our feelings of deprivation that make us want to "have it all."

For a mission president's wife, transfers are the most difficult assignment. Thirty-six times—every month for three years—she goes through it, and if she thought about them all at once, she probably couldn't get through the first one. For part of my mission I had household help, but for part of it I was on my own (as far as human help was concerned). For me it meant going with my husband to pick up our new group of missionaries (anywhere from six to twenty-six) at the airport when they arrived on a Tuesday about dinnertime. We could never guess just how long it would take to get through immigration, so we were to be gone from the house for an undetermined length of time. Nevertheless, within about ten minutes after we got home, a special welcoming dinner had to be on the table for the new missionaries and some of the office staff. For so large a group and with literally no last-minute time and no ability to know in advance the hour of the meal, I had a tall order to fill.

Immediately after dinner and rudimentary clearing of the table, the group would go downstairs to have a testimony meeting. It's an emotional time. New missionaries are frightened and in need of support. We would try to give such support as was needed, then settle them down for the night. Some hadn't read the list of what they were supposed to pack in the bag they bring into the mission home. There was always a considerable amount of last-minute confusion, but ultimately the missionaries were (figuratively) tucked in, and I could go downstairs and do the dishes and set up for breakfast before going to bed. The next morning there was breakfast, orientation (where I was assigned to teach a scripture workshop), lunch, assignments to areas, and farewells. Teary but full of hope, they listened to our encouraging tales of their new companions and areas, and then they were gone.

Before the last "greenie" was out of the mission home, the first of the departing missionaries arrived for their farewell. Worn-out suits; holes or patches in their parkas; hair cut by a companion or a nonprofessional local member, a little less sharp looking. More frightened to leave then than they had been to arrive two years before. Their "mission" was now awaiting them back home—and that place in Utah, or California, or Arizona had become foreign territory to them after eighteen months or two years as full-time missionaries. Some of them cried a lot that afternoon. All of them needed more support than they could get in their hour or so with the president for their departure interview. Somehow I managed to come through with a special dinner for their farewell that evening, the counseling and support in which I spent the afternoon notwithstanding. Not to mention that somewhere in there, I found the time to wash all the previous night's sheets, see that the new missionaries had made up the beds, and check that the bathrooms were in order.

That night after dinner there was the testimony meeting with the departing missionaries—again an emotional drain—and most of them couldn't get to sleep afterward. As I had in the old days when our adolescent children were still home, I sat up and talked with some of the departing missionaries.

The mission van arrived at five o'clock the next morning to take them to the airport, and I was usually still in my robe in the mission home driveway, giving them the only hug they'd had in two years. I always went back into the house crying. They were like my own, and some of them I would never see again.

As soon as they drove away, the president went quickly to his office—packing to leave on a zone conference round and encouraging me to get the linens washed quickly so that we could be on the way to Ottawa.

I tell you these details so that you can know my emotional and physical state as we took the two-and-a-half-hour drive to Ontario. I would have liked then to lay my head back and sleep. But my husband always prepared a stack of missionary letters for us to read together in the car as we drove. He would need to think about them before going into interviews that evening.

By the time we pulled into the hotel parking lot in Ottawa on those Wednesday nights, I was exhausted. So was my husband, of course, but he has more stamina than I have, and besides, more of what he did was sitting-down stuff. We checked in and took our things upstairs. There, in the middle of the room, was the most beautiful sight I would ever see: a bed. Rarely has anything been more inviting. But my husband was to leave in twenty minutes for the meetinghouse where he would interview missionaries. And my only opportunity to get to know missionaries was by visiting with them while companions were being interviewed. I could choose to stay at the hotel and get the needed rest, or I could choose to go to the meetinghouse and further my relationships with missionaries.

Relationships are one great blessing that the mission president's wife receives in her three years, and they don't happen automatically. She's got to have time to develop them. But after transfers I was *so* tired. If I chose to go to bed instead of accompanying my husband (and he left it up to me entirely), there would be eight missionaries whom I might not visit with for a total of three months. They're only out in the field twenty-two months. For the sister missionaries, time is even shorter. To miss a visit with them is to leave a pretty big hole in a relationship. What to choose? This one was not so easy. On the one side was a blessing I dearly desired, on the other a blessing I dearly needed.

If I went to bed after our arrival and slept through till the next morning, I would be rested the next day at the zone conference. At zone conferences I was assigned workshops, the quality of which would be seriously in question if I were worn out.

Another consideration is that a mission is a demanding

time in general. Health issues arise. The Lord expects us to take care of ourselves. Does it change things to know that I have some health problems—that I've had a stroke and sometimes drag around my left side when I overdo and don't get rest?

On the other hand, the relationships were a mutually exclusive blessing. If I didn't spend the time, I couldn't have the connection, no matter how righteous my intentions. What to choose?

Even those of us who have the scriptures for our guide find it difficult to believe that we can't "have it all." They're both righteous desires, right? If I go tonight, God will make me fresh in the morning with only a few hours' sleep. Or if I sleep tonight, God will make those missionaries feel close to me anyway. Right? I don't think so.

Oh, certainly he *can* do that. I believe that there are even times he *will* do that. But we mustn't assume it. The purpose of this life, after all, is to learn to choose correctly, to learn to choose in any given circumstance. If, whenever it got tough, he let us "have it all," if we did not exclude any other blessing by choosing the one we wanted, then where would be the development? Where would be the sacrifice? Where would be the revelation of the heart? Ultimately, where would be the blessings of heaven?

It's so easy when the right choice is obvious: save a life, accept a call. What about me and my little choice? What was the best choice in my case? Does what I choose even matter to the Lord? We see more than one instance in the scriptures where the Lord tells us that certain choices "mattereth not" to him (see D&C 27:2; 62:5; 80:3).

Nevertheless, whether the Lord had a special reason for my going to the meetinghouse on a given night or whether the choice was entirely up to me, I know that almost certainly

I could not expect to have the blessings on both sides of the coin. I would receive only the blessing I chose. So which was the more important blessing to choose? Which would bring me more desirable rewards? Sleep or visits? Rest or relationships? It was a difficult dilemma.

I believe that *only the Spirit can give us the answers we need to make life's choices.* Whether a choice matters to the Lord or matters only to ourselves, only the Spirit can tell us which choice is the better one, or which blessing will lead us more surely in the path of eternal life, or even which blessing (perhaps between equals as far as righteousness is concerned) may be the more rewarding for us (see 2 Ne. 32:3, 5; D&C 46:7). And true as that fact is, experiencing direction from the Spirit sounds easier than it actually is. Perhaps we sometimes tell ourselves it is the Spirit guiding us when it is only that our own preference is too strong for us to care. There may be times when we deny the Spirit because we're *afraid* our own preference may be too strong. Sometimes, for reasons known only to the Lord, the Spirit is withheld from us and we are on our own with our decisions. Everyone who strives for righteousness struggles for reassurance. Most often we must make our decisions based on righteous principles and wait upon the Lord for his ratification.

There is, however, a great and important secret: when we truly want God's will more than we want our own (or in other words, when we have our heart perfect before him)—when we truly trust him—his guidance will be much more available to us. What exactly should we sacrifice in this life in order to seek first the kingdom of heaven and its righteousness so that *ultimately* all else will be added unto us? It is my experience and it is my testimony that the Lord will tell us, when with all our hearts we truly seek him. It may come as direction—perhaps from the scriptures, or from our priesthood leaders, or even occasionally into our mind directly. It may come as ratification—perhaps recognizable in result, or perhaps in a flood of peace. But if we are seeking to meet his needs, the reassurance will be there for us—both for things little and for things large. Both for things obvious and things less apparent.

We spend this life choosing between mutually exclusive blessings—*not* having it all. It is myth to believe that if we make the "right" choice we get to have them both. We do not pay our tithing so that we can have the money. We do not get married in the temple in order to have the same joy that we would receive from having our nonmember family and friends present. We simply choose different joys. It is not "choose the right door and get the prizes behind all three." It is choose the right door and get the most important prize. That is the meaning, I think, of President McKay's statement "No other success can compensate for failure in the home."[3] That is a statement of fact, not of threat. Home is the most important choice. We choose among mutually exclusive blessings. We are not free to choose to receive blessings that exclude one another. Just as we are not free to choose reality.

So what did I choose? Sometimes I chose the meetinghouse. Sometimes the hotel. I wish I could report that in each case I sought the counsel or the will of the Lord and did it. Unfortunately, it was most often just my preference based on the profundity of my fatigue or the state of my health. It may have also been the Lord's will, or perhaps it mattered not to him at all. But I will never know, because most of those Wednesday nights my heart was not perfect enough to be visited with either direction or ratification. I know only that there were different blessings at the meetinghouse than there

---

3. President David O. McKay, "To the Parents in the Church," *Family Home Evening Manual 1968–69* (Salt Lake City: The Church of Jesus Christ of Latter-day Saints, 1967), iii.

were if I stayed behind and rested. In each case I received the blessings that I obviously valued more highly at the moment. I should also report to you that on none of the occasions did I receive both sets of blessings. They were indeed mutually exclusive.

As I learn to live gratefully with eternal perspective and to understand the nature of my eternal agency, I come closer to losing my natural feelings of deprivation. I come closer to seeing the blessings of heaven that sacrifice brings forth to me. I see that choices must be real and meaningful between mutually exclusive blessings and therefore cannot lead to "having it all." I see that believing in the possibility of having it all leads not to peace but to frustration.

Why should I be deprived? Because I want the peace of knowing what it is in life that is worthy of sacrifice—a complex question that has only a spiritual and experiential answer. I will surely make mistakes in knowing as I go along *what* to sacrifice. Perfection is not of this world, but if I reject sacrifice itself, believing that choice—and therefore deprivation—is unnecessary and valueless, I will fail in the educational purpose of this life. I testify that "sacrifice brings forth the blessings of heaven."

"Let us here observe, that a religion that does not require the sacrifice of all things never has power sufficient to produce the faith necessary unto life and salvation."[4]

"We look upon it as sacrifice. In its ultimate result, it proves to be not a sacrifice but a blessing."[5]

---

4. Joseph Smith Jr., *Lectures on Faith* (Salt Lake City: Deseret Book Co., 1985), 69.

5. Antoine R. Ivins, Report of the 123d Semiannual Conference of The Church of Jesus Christ of Latter-day Saints, October 1952, 19.

PART 5

Additional Thoughts

CHAPTER 13

Professional Help

Obviously there are times when the "love delivery" system (or the "love collection" system) goes awry and the ability to cope goes awry with it. Not to mention the times when the body's chemistry is faulty and interferes with our physical energy, our sense of reality, or our state of well-being. At these times, professional help can be a precious blessing. It can provide a troubled individual with a sense of security—even love. It can serve as a mirror with a reflection of our behavior patterns and the role those behaviors play in reinforcing our trouble. It can encourage us to find the strength to change those behaviors. It can help us understand the hearts and souls of other human beings. Medications can relieve us from physiological hindrances. All of these things and many more truly valuable helps can be found in the office of a mental health professional.

I believe in professional help. I endorse it. I recommend it. I'm grateful for the individuals who have chosen to give us of their love and patience.

Furthermore, psychotherapy can be consistent with the

Lord's way of blessing us. When accomplished by the proper therapist, it is one-on-one feeding of the sheep. It is helping another bear his burdens that they may be light.

With all that said, however, I must say that with many of our therapists there are elements that are *not* consistent with the scriptural instruction books for human development. It is not uncommon for a therapist to teach self-love—not just a semantic error meaning gratitude for one's being, but true self-love. These therapists teach love for self above others, giving only when "the bucket is full." This worldly philosophy is in complete contradiction to Paul's admonition to esteem others above ourselves (see Philip. 2:3).

The truth is that the search for a full bucket will never be ended. Everyone has an insatiable bucket as long as he is concentrating on it. We are not intended to meet all of our own needs. The scriptures teach the true reality that love is a long-handled spoon. The Golden Rule is all about concentrating on the needs of others, not of ourselves—for that is what we would truly have others do for us. The Christian paradox is a miracle. In direct proportion to our efforts to shake off our self-consciousness, our self-awareness, we will feel the Lord's love, and peace will descend.

It is also not uncommon for a therapist to teach a concentration on our victimhood. Looking for someone to blame is counterproductive because it uses energy that we could otherwise use much more profitably to do all that we can, without checklisting, and thereby grow. We are victims all. That is the truth of it. We need to acknowledge that, see the reality of it, and then forgive those who have victimized us and move on in a productive grateful way.

Only a therapist who understands (and in essence teaches) the Atonement can help us see that our victims' rights are satisfied by the gift we receive from God the Father:

the sacrifice of the Son of God. Because of that gift—that satisfaction of all victims' rights—we can release all blame.

A therapist, like anyone else who gives help to the distressed, should teach that our own guilt after repentance is also unnecessary because the price has been paid for our errors. What we are right now is unimportant because we have infinite potential if we just do all we can. Forgiveness will free us from the bondage of hate. Even if we wanted to, we could never fully pay the price for error as our Savior and Redeemer has done. Only a god could make that atonement. And God the Son has indeed made it.

There are some therapists who see that we cannot pay the price and therefore do indeed try to relieve our guilt. They may not, however, see that the reason guilt can be expunged is because it can lead to repentance and thus to relief through Him who paid the price. They do not see that Christ has atoned, and so they try to have their patients relieve their guilt unilaterally, unconditionally. These are the champions of self-esteem as a right. But each of us has in our very core an understanding of the law of justice, and without an understanding of the law of mercy as well, there is something inside of us that will not let go of the sense of guilt. Only when we learn to lay our burden on the Lord can we really set it down. It is not a matter of forgiving ourselves. It is a matter of accepting the Lord's forgiveness. For that reason, confidence must be a by-product of virtue and will be slow in coming because perfection is not of this world (see D&C 121:45).

Professional help is potentially so valuable. That is why it is important for us to understand that it is not true that a therapist is a therapist is a therapist. We can be and must be discriminating on the basis of a therapist's goals for us. The scriptures must be our guide as to what goals will be for our profit and long-term peace. Sometimes, in the depths of our distress, we may need spiritual guidance from a priesthood leader to see if our therapist's goals are consistent with the gospel of Jesus Christ. The peace that God offers is not "as the world giveth" (John 14:27). It is, however, profound. It is the peace that passeth understanding.

Professional help, like self-help, must lead to divine help if it is ever to produce its promise of peace. The arm of flesh is flabby. It cannot, unaided, make us to lie down in green pastures beside the still waters.

CHAPTER 14

For Moms and Dads

Recently a friend whom I had been badgering with anti–self-esteem rhetoric said to me, "Okay, you've convinced me. I see that I need to raise humble kids. But it's hard. My daughter is so intelligent, so beautiful, so accomplished. I just hate ignoring all that. My heart bursts to tell her how proud I am of her."

"Don't restrain yourself," I said. "Tell her. Tell her with all the fervor of your soul. Your pride is born of your love for her. Express it! By all means express it!"

I thought instantly of Alma declaring his love for Shiblon: "I say unto you, my son, that I have had great joy in thee already, because of thy faithfulness and thy diligence" (Alma 38:3).

"But I don't want to create a 'compliment junkie,'" my friend responded. "You've got me scared."

That was not my intent, and I have since given a great deal of thought to the delicate balancing act a parent must master. I want to comfort others, not pressure them, by expressing my thoughts about the challenges of self-esteem. What I want to say to parents is, Let your child know that you are grateful for her, that you are grateful for each and every gift she has. Teach her that she must be grateful for them, too. Help her remember that "every good gift and every perfect gift is from above, and cometh down from the Father of lights" (James 1:17). The Lord himself said it best to the ancient children of Israel: "And thou shalt rejoice in every good thing which the Lord thy God hath given unto thee, and unto thine house, thou, and the Levite, and the stranger that is among you" (Deut. 26:11).

I believe the best motto is *Rejoice but don't flatter.* It is an underlying difference in goal. Rejoicing is looking for ways to express your delight in your child. Flattery is looking for ways to make your child feel good about himself. The contrast is in whether you are genuinely expressing *your* feelings or trying to influence *his* feelings. It is a subtle but crucial difference. Chances are that your children will understand which of the two feelings is motivating your praise.Your intent will show.

What you feel inside will determine whether you are giving your child joyful love or addictive praise. We sometimes need to change focus with our children. Once their search for self-esteem is no longer important to us, once we care only about loving them, being kind to them, rejoicing in them, and teaching them to get their confidence from the Lord—then communication can become freer and more open. And, I might add, that communication has more credibility to the child. Praise that is an expression of gratitude to the Lord, "a joyful noise to the rock of our salvation" (Ps. 95:1), is part of a warm, loving environment. Praise that is designed to require of the child that she feel good about herself is anxiety producing. What we say comes naturally out of us when we are clear on our purpose.

Actually, where praise is concerned it is not so difficult to make the focus change. The real difficulty usually arises not when the child brings joy but when the child brings pain or disappointment—either to the parent or to himself. In these times of stress, it is easiest to revert to our natural man: that part of us that wants to attend to the comfort of the moment and is willing to do so with flattery—or that part of us that lashes out at the child with criticism. When we are discomfited it takes all our strength to think in terms of the long-range view. But it is that perspective that will stop us from making errors.

I remember when one of my sons returned home from his first grade class in tears because he had been changed from the advanced to the middle reading group. I have a vivid memory of pulling him onto my lap and holding him. I wanted to cry with him. Mercifully, my memory ends there. I suspect that I pointed out to him that he had many other areas in which he excelled, or told him that he was a wonderful reader and I thought the teacher was crazy. Flattery was my style in those days. Interesting, isn't it, that my memory is of the love I felt for him? I only hope that his memory is the same. How much better off I would have been to follow the advice of Paul to the Romans: "Let love be without dissimulation . . . rejoicing in hope; patient in tribulation; Rejoice with them that do rejoice, and weep with them that weep" (Rom. 12:9, 12, 15). Empathy and hope were needed, not a more intense self-focus. The perspective of thirty-some-odd years has taught me that, sure enough, he had time enough to learn to read. He didn't have to be the best reader in the first grade.There are no clocks in the garden.

As natural men we want to reassure with "Don't worry; you're wonderful." I think the more helpful reassurance would be "Don't worry about being wonderful."

"Oh, Sweetheart," I might have said to my little first grader, had I had the vision to see the end in the beginning, "life can be so unhappy sometimes. I wish it weren't so, but it just is." And then later, when he was comforted enough to plan to achieve what he wanted, then comes the teaching moment: "I know you want to be the very best right now. That's what we all want. But honestly, darling, 'now' isn't that important. You will learn to read. You can do anything well that you keep working at. Heavenly Father has promised us that. I love that you want it that badly. I love that reading is important to you. It fills my heart with pride. Oh, how lucky I am to have you. What a wonderful blessing you are to me." I could have helped him to state confidently, as did the Apostle Paul, "I can do all things through Christ which strengtheneth me" (Philip. 4:13).

The same response is needful to the child who has made mistakes. We may even have to point out those mistakes, because until the child feels the pain of having done the wrong thing, there is little we can do. But when the pain is intense, we must reassure, with understanding and empathy, that we know that life's tribulation is difficult to bear. Then, when the comfort of that empathy is achieved, we can teach about the Atonement and the potential for overcoming the pain of this world. "These things I have spoken unto you, that in me ye might have peace," said the Savior of the world to the sorrowing apostles. "In the world ye shall have tribulation: but be of good cheer; I have overcome the world" (John 16:33). Our teaching must always include getting our strength from God and keeping the commandments. I can think of no mistake so small that the sorrow for it should not be met by the parent with teaching of the Atonement and the hope that is in it.

"Rejoice with them that do rejoice and weep with them that weep" (Rom. 12:15). Teach your children to get their strength from God and to keep the commandments. That is what matters.

We live in a society that is saturated with the worldly view. The search for self-esteem is widely used as a substitute for the Savior's atonement. Teachers, programs, and friends will engage in well-intentioned flattery and its resulting encouragement of self-focus. Our children must live in that world.

We may ask ourselves, Even if I change my own focus, will that be enough to spare my children the blame and insatiability trap? My answer is an emphatic YES! It is the same as rearing your children with an understanding of the other facets of the gospel of Jesus Christ. Many of us have reared or are rearing Mormon children in a non-LDS environment. Our children show their strength when they don't partake of those things that are contrary to their faith. They receive the security in their beliefs at home, and it is an indication of their courage and uniqueness when they don't violate those beliefs even when they're away from home. They know, at a surprisingly young age, where to get illegal drugs, for instance; but they resist, and they "just say no" when drugs are offered to them. They live in the world but not of the world. It can be the same as we help our children resist the stressful search for self-esteem and seek the peace of the gospel instead.

But there will be people in the family or members of the Church who will give them that "search for self-esteem" drug. Doesn't that make it tougher? Yes, it does. But ultimately, their security base, their value system, will arm them with the ability to withstand addictive behaviors of all kinds. Love will strengthen them.

I remember once, at a medical society banquet in California, the speaker was giving statistics about drug use at our universities. He quoted the pitifully small percentage of students at Stanford who had not at least tried illegal drugs. Then he said, "And in that tiny percentage you have to remember there are a significant number of Mormons—who have principles about it. They don't even drink coffee."

I am suggesting that children who have been raised by parents who love them, rejoice with them, weep with them, teach them patience and diligence and dependence upon their Father in Heaven—parents who teach their children to be humble and realistic and hopeful will have children who (barring only their own choice to do otherwise) will find peace.

"The Lord thy God in the midst of thee is mighty; he will save, he will rejoice over thee with joy; he will rest in his love, he will joy over thee with singing" (Zeph. 3:17).

"Yea, and [ye] are willing to mourn with those that mourn: yea, and comfort those that stand in need of comfort, and to stand as witnesses of God at all times and in all things" (Mosiah 18:9).

"And see that all these things are done in wisdom and order; for it is not requisite that a man should run faster than he has strength. And again, it is expedient that he should be diligent, that thereby he might win the prize" (Mosiah 4:27).

CHAPTER 15

Hope—
The Power to Change Our Focus

There is hope in recognizing the limits of our adequacy in contrast to our Father in Heaven and our Savior Jesus Christ. There is great comfort in the Lord's reminder that there is none good but God (see Mark 10:18). There would be despair in believing that it doesn't get any better than all of us know we are. The knowledge that there exists a being who is mightier than all the earth, that he is our Father and that he loves us, that we are not limited by our own being—this is all a source of inestimable hope. We are like little children who could not survive on our own. But our great and mighty Father has provided us with his knowledge in the form of commandments, and his promise that if we obey them, he will bless us with more commandments through the Spirit (see D&C 59:4). As if that weren't enough, he has provided us with, first, an atonement so that our errors, both petty and grand, will not hold us back and, second, the security of knowing that at the end of our trials, through the astonishing love of our birthright elder brother, a home with God awaits us. What more hope can we have than love, guidance, and the Atonement?

It is hope that has within it the power to change our focus to peace from pride.

C. S. Lewis in *Mere Christianity* said, "In God you come up against something which is in every respect immeasurably superior to yourself. Unless you know God as that—and therefore, know yourself as nothing in comparison—you do not know God at all."[1]

It is a restatement, of course, of the great truth taught by King Benjamin: "I would that ye should remember and always retain in remembrance, the greatness of God and your own nothingness and his goodness and long-suffering towards you" (Mosiah 4:11).

At the point of understanding this principle, we arrive where Nephi seems to have started out: "Let us be faithful in keeping the commandments of the Lord; for behold he is mightier than all the earth" (1 Ne. 4:1).

Those commandments that Nephi exhorts us to keep sometimes seem difficult. If we focus on our performance, they seem downright impossible. We must focus instead on our effort, on our sacrifice, on our hearts being right with our Father in Heaven, because then, and only then, will we feel hopeful when our performance flags and comforted when our limits become obvious. When our hearts are committed to the Lord, we will work with all of our might, mind, and strength, for his objectives, and will be blessed with peace.

Joseph Smith said, "Let the Saints remember that great things depend on their individual exertion, and that they are called to be co-workers with us and the Holy Spirit in accom-

---

1. C. S. Lewis, *Mere Christianity* (New York: Simon & Schuster, 1996), 111.

plishing the great work of the last days: and in consideration of the extent, the blessings and glories of the same, let every selfish feeling be not only buried, but annihilated; and let love to God and man predominate, and reign triumphant in every mind, that their hearts may become like unto Enoch's of old, and comprehend all things, present, past and future, and come behind in no gift, waiting for the coming of the Lord Jesus Christ."[2]

What a contrast that is to the philosophies of men. It is not "peace made simple"; it is "peace made exertion." And yet, it is simpler than their way. What beautiful irony. Men give us "something we can do," and we end up unable to do enough of it. God asks of us unmeasured exertion, and it ends up something we can do.

No wonder we find hope there. It starts with the hope of humility and ends with the hope of rebirth. It is in hope that the power rests.

Self-esteem will never work as a substitute for the Atonement. Only Jesus Christ, the Son of God, will truly give us the power and strength and peace we long for. That peace or confidence is the by-product of putting aside our self-awareness in total heartfelt obedience to our Father in Heaven. It is the process of abasing ourselves in order to be exalted. Self-abasement is the ironic root of peace. Hope is what makes it possible. Herein is hope: The power to change through Christ.

Brigham Young taught the Saints, "We have brought the doctrine of life and salvation to you, that you may exchange your low, narrow, contracted, selfish dispositions for the ennobling Spirit of the Lord, for the Spirit of the Gospel,

---

2. *Teachings of the Prophet Joseph Smith* (Salt Lake City: Deseret Book Co., 1976), 178–79.

which gives joy and peace. If you enjoy that, your food will be sweet to you, your sleep will be refreshing, and your days will pass away in usefulness."[3]

---

3. *Journal of Discourses* 3:119, as quoted in *Discourses of Brigham Young,* comp. John A. Widtsoe (Salt Lake City: Deseret Book Co., 1954), 6.

Index